PREFACE

From 1946 until 1984 approximately 150,000 Mediterranean tortoises were imported each year into the United Kingdom. Similar numbers were imported into other northern European countries, making a probable total of about 6,000,000 into the U.K. and about 20,000,000 into northern Europe as a whole. M. R. K. Lambert, P. W. P. Collins, and K. Lawrence in England, Blatt and Muller in Germany, and others have carried out extensive work to find out how many tortoises have survived the experience. The general conclusions of all these workers are:

1) Approximately 80% of tortoises moved die or are lost within one year.

2) Although some individuals live a considerable time, the average time spent in northern Europe before death is less than three years.

3) Hatchlings born in northern Europe fare no better, their average life span also under three years.

This book tries to explain why. It is intended to be read and understood by the many tortoise owners in northern Europe, hence I have avoided scientific language as much as possible. I have mixed experimental data and theories derived from them. I have not given full references to all the sources of information. I hope that any scientist reading this will understand my reasons and will not reject the science contained here because of the way it is expressed.

Most of the experimental work has been done on a very broad front in order to try to obtain an overall picture of the strategies these animals use for survival, and hence a comprehensive picture of the strategies necessary for keepers to use in order to keep and breed them successfully over extended periods.

In the last five years enormous strides have been taken in the understanding of tortoise husbandy. I am aware that much of the advice offered in this book differs sharply from that given in books published ten years ago. I am also aware that over the next few years further improvements in understanding are likely to modify some of the advice contained here. There is huge scope for detailed research in every aspect of this field.

However, in spite of this proviso, I can almost guarantee that any tortoise keepers changing from previously accepted methods of husbandry to those advocated here will experience a dramatic change in general health, life expectancy, level of activity, and general appearance of their charges.

This is a *big claim!*
Test it!

Testudo graeca juvenile. Photo by W. P. Mara.

DEDICATION

This book is dedicated to the following tortoises that paid the ultimate price—their lives—for the knowledge that is in these pages.

Philip, a *Testudo hermanni* male, who died of anorexia (starvation) in April, 1979. His death brought me to the uneasy conclusion that all the husbandry literature available at the time was inadequate and that general veterinary advice and care available at the time were insufficient to compensate. His death marked the first step in a ten-year struggle to find out how to keep tortoises fit and healthy.

Lilly, a *Testudo graeca ibera* female, who died of egg peritonitis in March, 1987. Her death and subsequent post-mortem opened my eyes to the miracles

and the potentially lethal dangers of tortoise reproduction.

Timmy, a *Testudo graeca terrestris* male, who died from septicaemia after first suffering from a flagellate infestation. His death taught me about disease progression and the importance of early and accurate diagnosis and appropriate treatment.

EDITORIAL NOTE

The observations and interpretations presented here are those of the author and may be found to apply only to very specific captive care situations in Great Britain. Experience may show that some interpretations and suggestions will not apply in other parts of the world and to other species.

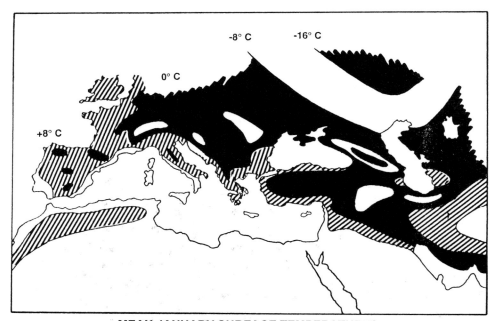

MEAN JANUARY SURFACE TEMPERATURES
There is a widespread misconception that the winter in the British Isles is comparatively cold because it gets colder the further north you travel. Although this is very true of summer temperatures, the winter temperatures decrease in Europe from west to east, making English winters comparatively mild.

ZOOGEOGRAPHY & EVOLUTION

There are a variety of factors that influence the distribution of tortoises in the wild. The most important of these are ambient air temperatures, annual hours of sunshine, availability of calcium carbonate, availability of suitable food, and activities of mankind. Factors of lesser importance include altitude, predators, and competitors.

AIR TEMPERATURE

Air temperature is of vital importance to tortoises that are native to tropical forest areas that require a steady day/night and summer/winter temperature of 26°C to 30°C (79°F to 86°F). Mediterranean tortoises, in contrast, have evolved various strategies for coping with inappropriate temperatures. However, air temperatures between -5°C and +5°C (23°F and 41°F) are appropriate to enable the tortoise to achieve its correct body temperature of 4°C to 5°C (39°F to 41°F)* while hibernating. Air temperatures between 18°C and 28°C (65°F and 82°F) are appropriate to enable a body temperature of 30°C (86°F) to be achieved while the tortoise is awake. Mediterranean tortoises have problems if they have to endure temperatures higher, lower, or between these figures for extended periods. This means that geographical areas where the January/July temperature range is of the order of 25°C to 35°C (77°F to 95°F) are preferred. (The temperature in the U.K. is about 15°C [59°F].) Most residents of the U.K. seem to know that Mediterranean summers are warmer than English summers, but few seem to realise that inland Mediterranean winters are colder than English winters.

American towns with climates approximating that of the climate of the home ranges of *Testudo graeca* and *Testudo hermanni* are New York, Toledo, and St. Louis. The nearest equivalent to the English climate in the USA is Seattle.

SUNSHINE

Mediterranean tortoises use sunshine directly or indirectly at all stages of their life cycle. They need at least 2,500 hours of sunshine per year in order to exist on a long term basis. In Europe and North Africa, annual sunshine hours reduce from south to north. Wild tortoises do not exist north of a line marking a light level of 2,500 hours per year.

CALCIUM

For most of the time between 340,000,000 BC, and 40,000,000 BC, what are now Europe and North Africa were tropical rainforest and in the area between the two was a large tropical sea called the Tethys Sea. The sea became very shallow with the build up of coral and algae remains. Shallow tropical seas evaporate rapidly, becoming very salty. Calcium salts normally dissolved in the water then are deposited on the bottom. Over a period of 300,000,000 years these deposits became a bed of limestone (calcium carbonate) thousands of feet thick covering a huge area.

Subsequent buckling of the earth's surface has turned these deposits into the Atlas Mountains in Morocco and Algeria, the Dolomites in Yugoslavia, and the limestone plateau of Turkey. This limestone fills the need that tortoises have for a raw material from which to encourage the growth of their bones, claws, scales, carapaces, and plastrons.

There are other calcium-rich areas in the Mediterranean region. In Tunisia and in Southwest Asia there are internal drainage basins where rivers full of calcium washed from the limestone uplands evaporate to leave deposits rich in calcium.

Tortoises live only in calcium-rich areas. For example, Portugal, with a perfectly adequate climate but no limestone, has no wild tortoises.

AVAILABILITY OF FOOD

Although the tortoises can exist in areas with very little food, there obviously is a minimum limit. The deserts of Arabia, the Negev, and the Sahara mark the southern boundaries of the tortoises's domain. Most climatic maps use the "under 10 inches (25 cm) of rain" line to

Recently I've come to believe that about 5°C (41°F) is best.

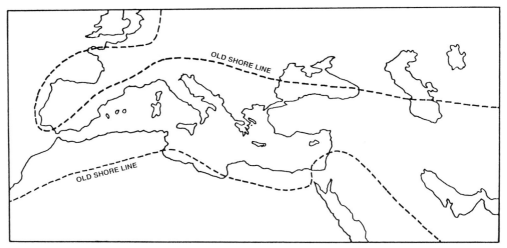

HYPOTHETICAL MAP OF THE TETHYS SEA

The Tethys Sea existed from 340,000,000 years to 40,000,000 years ago, going through slow evolutionary changes during this 300,000,000 year period. Since tortoises only occur in calcium-rich areas, they have been restricted to the calcium deposits laid down millions of years ago by the Tethys Sea evaporations.

ANNUAL HOURS OF SUNSHINE

Tortoises in the wild do not live north of the line marking 2500 hours of sunshine per year.

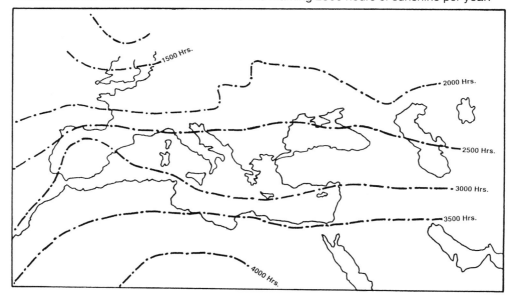

mark the edge of a desert. Mediterranean tortoises can exist in areas with less rainfall than this, probably down to about 5 inches (12.5 cm) per year.

ACTIVITIES OF MANKIND

Mankind uses potential tortoise habitats for towns and intensive agriculture, leaving in general only barren upland areas for the tortoise. One effect of this that often is overlooked is that, with the valleys often barred by human activity, upland tortoises can become isolated and hence inbred.

Some agricultural methods, particularly burning fields and using chemical sprays, can do considerable damage. For much of the past 50 years, Mediterranean tortoises were collected for pets and transported to northern Europe in ever-increasing numbers until 1977, when the Russians banned the export of *Testudo horsfieldi* from Russia, and 1984, when most Mediterranean species were included in the C.I.T.E.S. agreement. At the time of writing, tortoises in Morocco are still killed to make into tourist souvenirs.

In general, tortoises, in common with most other wild animals, have considerable survival problems when they come into contact with mankind.

ALTITUDE

Tortoises cannot exist past the snow line on high mountains. There are several ranges of mountains that form an effective barrier to tortoise travel. It is, of course, not the altitude that stops them but the fact that the air temperature falls along with the altitude. These barriers have a significant effect on tortoise speciation.

PREDATORS

Adult tortoises have virtually no predators unless you count mankind. However, eggs and hatchlings can be predated by animals such as rats. The tortoise avoids this problem by laying, on average, two and a half batches of eggs per year with an average number of six eggs per batch, so that some losses are acceptable.

COMPETITORS

Many animals such as rabbits and goats compete with the tortoise for food supplies. When the climate is difficult, mammals, with their fur coats and built-in heating, have the upper hand, but in areas where the climate is right but food and water are scarce, the tortoise can exist happily where mammals starve. This is because tortoises don't waste water in perspiration or urination, and don't waste food supplying body heat.

EVOLUTION

Mediterranean (hibernating) tortoises have evolved from tropical (non-hibernating) tortoises. They originally lived on the northern fringes of tropical forests, but the shrinking of the area of rainforests and the formation and growth of deserts such as the Sahara have separated the two types. More recent geological events, in particular the formation by surface folding of the mountain ranges around the Mediterranean and the flooding of the basin to form the Mediterranean Sea, have had the effect of physically separating groups of tortoises. These separated groups then gradually develop differing characteristics. This process is called speciation. If the differences are large enough to prevent cross-breeding between groups, they are species differences. If the differences are enough to prevent most but not all cross-breeding, subspecific. If the differences are noticeable but cross-breeding occurs regularly, the differences are racial.

Because of the way tortoises breed, it is not easy to find out how group differences should be classified. This has led to some divergence of opinion among zoologists concerning the naming of the various groups of Mediterranean tortoises. This book uses the most commonly accepted taxonomy (method of naming), but it is important to realise that other authors may use different names to describe the same tortoises, and that one author might describe a difference as specific but another might describe the same difference as subspecific or even racial.

SPECIES & SEX RECOGNITION

ANATOMY

The upper shell of a tortoise is called the "carapace." The lower shell is called the "plastron." Both of these are divided into areas called "scutes." The posterior upper scute is called the "supracaudal" ("over the tail") scute. Some tortoises have modified scales either on the rear of their thighs or on the heels to provide added protection from would-be predators; these are called "spurs." An enlarged scale also may be present at the end of the tail. A weak, often barely visible, hinge divides the front and back lobes of the plastron in all species but *Testudo horsfieldi*. The front legs may have only four or five rows of large non-overlapping scales at the front or up to ten rows of smaller, more normal scales.

SPECIES RECOGNITION

There are five species of tortoise living in the Mediterranean region, and with careful examination it is not difficult to distinguish between them. It is important to realise that the differences between the species are equivalent to the differences between, for example, human beings and orangutans. Different species do not, as a rule, provide "good company" for each other.

Testudo graeca (Greek Tortoise).* First described by a Swedish botanist named Carolus Linnaeus in 1758. *Testudo* is the genus name. It is Latin and means "tortoise." *Graeca* is the species name; it is also Latin and means "Greek." However, this species rarely comes from Greece. Linnaeus gave them this name because he thought the pattern on their carapaces looked like a Greek mosaic. The name has been confusing tortoise fanciers ever since! This also is called the Spur-thighed Tortoise. Most of them were exported to northern Europe from Morocco or Turkey, and they formed the majority of the trade between 1946 and 1984. The natural range extends from Spain across northern Africa to the Middle East and Iran, up to

I really would prefer the name Spur-thighed Tortoise but have given up on changing entrenched usage.

the Balkans and northern Greece.

Testudo hermanni (Hermann's Tortoise). First described by Gmelin in 1789. *Hermanni* is the Latinisation of a zoologist's name. Large numbers were exported mainly from Yugoslavia. This cool-adapted tortoise occurs over much of southern Europe east to Turkey.

Testudo marginata (Margined Tortoise). First described by Schoepff in 1792. *Marginata* means "marginated" and refers to the crenellated shape of the rear edge of the adult's carapace. Their main range is restricted to southern Greece and the Greek Islands. They are the fastest growing of the Mediterranean tortoises.

Testudo horsfieldi (Horsfield's Tortoise). First described by Gray in 1844. This tortoise's natural home range is Afghanistan and southwestern Russia around the Caspian to Pakistan. Because these areas are subject to very hard winters with temperatures often dropping to well below freezing, these tortoises are agile and dig deeply for hibernation to avoid the winter frosts that would otherwise be lethal.

During the summer, the day temperatures in this region can become unacceptably high (over 86°F), and as a result these tortoises will burrow to avoid overheating. The effect of these strategies is that the tortoises commonly are seen on the surface for only about three months of the year, in spring and early summer.

Testudo kleinmanni (Egyptian Tortoise). First described by Lortet in 1883. The range of these tortoises is northern Africa from Libya to the Sinai. Although these tortoises have been anatomically well-described, very little about their habits has been published and they are rarely seen in northern Europe. Since the ambient temperature in Egypt rarely falls below 59°F, I assume that they do not normally hibernate.

SEX RECOGNITION

The majority of prior publications describe female tortoises of the genus *Testudo* as having a flat plastron and the males as having a concave plastron. This description is misleading, however. The

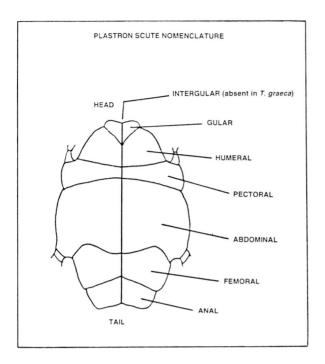

PLASTRON SCUTE NOMENCLATURE

HEAD

INTERGULAR (absent in *T. graeca*)

GULAR

HUMERAL

PECTORAL

ABDOMINAL

FEMORAL

ANAL

TAIL

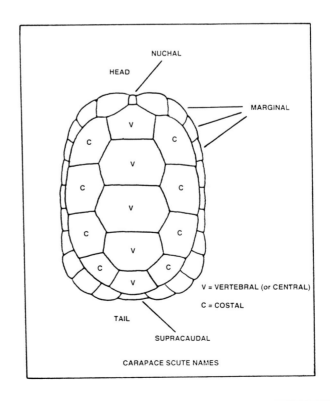

NUCHAL

HEAD

MARGINAL

V = VERTEBRAL (or CENTRAL)

C = COSTAL

TAIL

SUPRACAUDAL

CARAPACE SCUTE NAMES

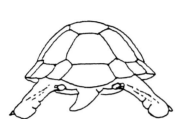
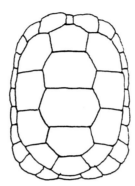
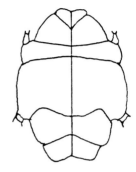

Testudo graeca

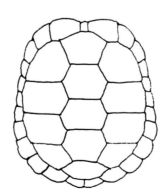
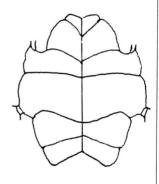

Testudo hermanni

HOW TO RECOGNIZE THE SPECIES OF *TESTUDO*

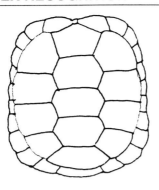 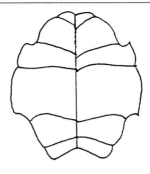

Testudo horsfieldi

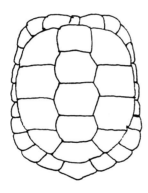 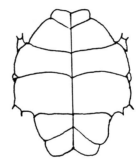

Testudo kleinmanni

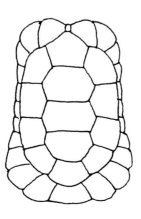 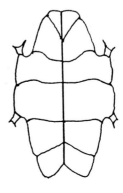

Testudo marginata

difference described is a secondary sexual characteristic.

Juvenile tortoises do not show any external sexual differences until they are four to six years old. Males kept as solitary animals during this transition period exhibit either no or very little characteristic concavity. The concavity appears to develop as a result of the persistent mounting of the female that is usual behaviour at this time.

The primary external sexual differences in the genus *Testudo* are tail shape and size. In *Testudo graeca* the female's tail is short (about one-fifth of the length of the back legs) and her vent is puckered, circular, and faces downward when the tail is held in line with the spine. Male tails are longer (about three-quarters of the length of the back legs), and the vent is a longitudinal slit that faces forward when the tail is held centrally.

There are other differences. Males normally carry their tails tucked up sideways. Females carry their tails sideways when hibernating, anorexic, or ill; at most other times they carry their tails centrally. The rear lobe of the plastron of adult female *T. graeca* is hinged to facilitate egglaying. The male and juvenile rear plastral lobe is sometimes rigid and sometimes very slightly flexible.

Occasionally the situation is more complicated. I have seen three examples of *T. graeca* that were imported before sexual maturity and, due to sub-optimal husbandry, had grown very little since their import. In each case the animal appeared to be a half-developed male with a tail one-half to two-thirds of the normal length. Even more surprising is an example where I have observed the male genitalia of a fully grown tortoise and have been assured by several different people that an X-ray exists showing eggs inside this particular tortoise!

GENUS *TESTUDO*: Species recognition details

Species:	graeca	hermanni	marginata	horsfieldi	kleinmanni
Thigh spurs:	yes	no	no	yes	no
Tail scale:	no	yes	no	yes	no
Hinged plastron:	adult females	no	no	no	both sexes
Forelimb scales:	3-7 rows large	5-10 rows small	4-5 rows large	5-6 rows large	3-4 rows large
Front claws:	5	5	5	4	5
Supracaudal scutes:	1	2	1	1	1
Nuchal scute:	narrow	narrow	narrow	small	wide

MEDITERRANEAN TORTOISE RANGES

This is a generalized map based upon reports of many investigators. Some of these reports were contradictory and the author relied in those cases on his own judgment. This pictorial does, however, give a good idea of the complexity of the distribution of Mediterranean tortoise populations.

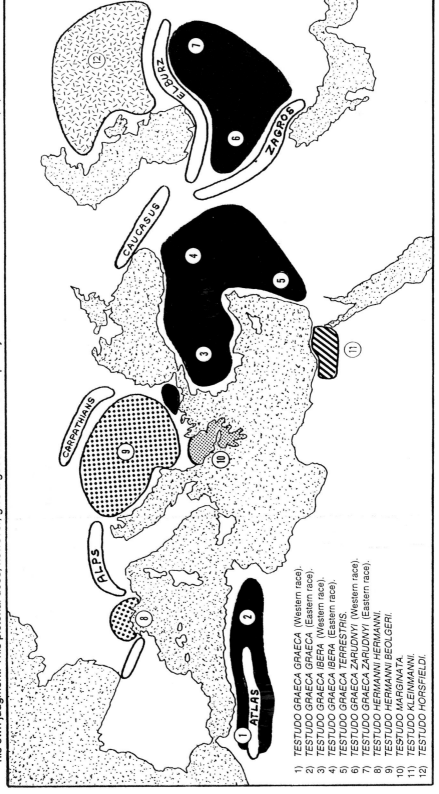

1) TESTUDO GRAECA GRAECA (Western race).
2) TESTUDO GRAECA GRAECA (Eastern race).
3) TESTUDO GRAECA IBERA (Western race).
4) TESTUDO GRAECA IBERA (Eastern race).
5) TESTUDO GRAECA TERRESTRIS.
6) TESTUDO GRAECA ZARUDNYI (Western race).
7) TESTUDO GRAECA ZARUDNYI (Eastern race).
8) TESTUDO HERMANNI HERMANNI.
9) TESTUDO HERMANNI BEOLGERI.
10) TESTUDO MARGINATA.
11) TESTUDO KLEINMANNI.
12) TESTUDO HORSFIELDI.

SUBSPECIES RECOGNITION

The species *Testudo graeca*, the animal that this book is primarily concerned with, exists in subtly different forms in various regions. Each form is adapted to the climate and vegetation of its own region. Breeding between individuals of one region is relatively straightforward (subject to getting conditions correct), but cross-breeding between regions is generally unsuccessful.

A word of warning—at the time of writing, insufficient zoological field work has been done for anyone to be sure about the extent of the areas occupied by all the types of tortoises described here, or for anyone to be sure if particular differences are specific, subspecific or racial. The naming system used here is that most generally used. It may or may not be scientifically correct. The only way to be sure is to carry out DNA analysis on tortoises from all the various areas. Time will tell. I feel that even if there are detail errors in this list, its publication is worthwhile because it provides a good picture of the complexity of the Mediterranean tortoise population and the care required when captive breeding.

The reader must be his or her own judge about this and alternative systems of naming suggested by other authors. However, be very wary about any differences described as specific or subspecific that use size as a comparison factor. Tortoise growth rates, and hence average sizes, are very dependent on diet and thermal husbandry.

Testudo graeca graeca (western race)
This normally is classified as the main or "nominate" subspecies. Its range is the slopes of the western Atlas Mountains in Morocco, North Africa.

Testudo graeca graeca (eastern race)
Range—Eastern Atlas Mountains in Algeria and parts of Tunisia and Libya.

Testudo graeca ibera (western race)
Range—Northern Greece and north-western Turkey. Note that "ibera" is a village in Turkey, and this turtle does not occur in Spain.

Testudo graeca ibera (eastern race)
Range—southeastern Turkey.

Testudo graeca terrestris
Range—Syria, Lebanon, and Israel.
Testudo graeca zarudnyi (eastern race)
Range—eastern Iran.
Testudo graeca zarudnyi (western race)
Range—western Iran.

The ranges listed above are the main areas, but to complicate the issue mankind has transported some animals from their previous habitats to new areas, where fresh colonies sometimes develop.

When attempting to identify to which group an individual specimen belongs, it must be realised that the external differences between the groups are quite subtle, but differences between individuals produced by sexual diversity can be very large. This means that regional differences can be masked. It is important to realise that the amount of melanism (black colouration) in the carapace is very variable and hence is a very poor indicator of regional origins. Also, size and rate of growth are very dependent on habitat and hence are useless as an indicator once the tortoise has been moved to a new habitat.

Before attempting to classify a tortoise, wash it thoroughly; this includes carapace, plastron, and body scales. It is impossible to judge subtle shadings beneath a layer of oil and grime. Look at *all* possible recognition features carefully; do not make a judgement on one feature only. If possible, compare the features with those of other tortoises. Known breeding pairs are very useful for comparison purposes; they can give one a feel for the variations and similarities possible within a subspecies.

RECOGNITION FEATURES
Eyebrow Ridges: *T. g. graeca* has high "frog-like" eyebrow ridges. All other subspecies have minimal "snake-like" ridges.

Claws: *T. g. graeca* and *T. g. ibera* have claws that shade from brownish at their base to parchment colour at their tips. *T. g. terrestris* front claws normally are parchment coloured; the outside two rear claws on each foot normally are dark brown, the inside rear claws are parchment-coloured. *T. g. zarudnyi* has all claws black or very dark brown.

Body Scale Colouration: All the legs, shoulders, head, neck, and hips that are visible between plastron and carapace are covered with scales. These scales vary in colouration. *T. g. graeca* scales are mostly parchment-coloured, but closer examination of the scales on the shoulders normally reveals that they are actually mottled yellow and brown. *T. g. ibera* scales are parchment-coloured. In *T. g. terrestris* the hind legs are light inside and dark outside, normally with a sharp division between the two tones. There normally are yellow markings on the sides and top of the head. *T. g. zarudnyi* has scales that are very dark over the whole of its body.

Carapace Shape: In *T. g. zarudnyi* (eastern race) the carapace becomes flared over the front and rear legs in adult specimens. Flaring is absent or minor in the other subspecies.

Carapace Melanin Patterns: *Testudo graeca* carapaces are divided into scutes. Each of these scutes has patterns of dark shading caused by the dark brown pigment melanin. The extent of dark coloration (melanism) varies from scute to scute and from tortoise to tortoise. It depends initially on parentage and is inherited, but it also varies with the tortoise's diet and state of health. However, there are certain broad similarities of pattern within the species as a whole and within each subgroup.

Each *Testudo graeca* scute has a basic dark pattern consisting of an outline on the front edge and top and bottom sides (a "C") and a central mark (a "dot").

T. g. graeca (west): The "C" is broken up or partly broken up in the form of dots, particularly on the costal scutes.

T. g. graeca (east): The "C" is broken up or partly broken up in the form of radial lines and dots.

T. g. ibera (west): Basic pattern.

T. g. ibera (east): The "C" is broken up to form radial lines.

T. g. terrestris: The "C" is sometimes in the form of radial lines, normally almost non-existent, leaving just a central mark.

T. g. zarudnyi: The "C" is extended to cover all or most of the scute.

Carapace Background Colour: In *T. g. graeca* there generally is a slight orange tinge to the background carapace colour. All other subspecies have a parchment-coloured background. The difference is very slight. It normally is necessary to have two tortoises side by side to appreciate the difference. As in all comparisons, don't be fooled by dirt, algae, oil, or shell rot.

Species recognition is easy and the differences are clearcut, but be warned, subspecies recognition takes practice. The differences frequently are not clearcut and it is easy to be wrong!

The differences in melanin patterns between the eastern and western Atlas *Testudo graeca* (and similarly the differences between eastern and western Turkish *Testudo graeca*) can be equated to climatic differences. The western regions have prevailing onshore winds and consequently higher rainfall than the eastern regions. This means that western shrub cover is predominantly round leaved, casting crescent-shaped shadows that match the dark carapace patterns when the tortoise hides. By contrast, in the drier eastern regions the shrub cover is predominantly spikey leaved, and the "starburst" patterns match their shadow shapes. Or at least that is one theory proposed to explain the differences.

TEMPERATURE CONTROL

Tortoises are reptiles. Human beings are mammals. One very significant difference between reptiles and mammals is the methods used to control body temperature. Humans and other mammals produce body heat by utilising the food they eat as fuel. They have internal regulation mechanisms to ensure that the body temperature remains more or less constant regardless of air temperature fluctuations. One may feel warm or cold, but this normally is a measure of heat gain or loss from the surroundings, not of body temperature. This is an automatic system that requires no conscious thought. Tortoises are different. Though they also require a steady, warm, body temperature because the delicate chemistry of animal life is upset if the temperature is incorrect, they do not have the internal mammalian systems to achieve this.

From the point of view of temperature control there are four types of tortoises.

Tropical Rainforest Tortoises

A tropical rainforest is a unique habitat for animals. The combination of overhead sun (similar day length at all times of the year), thick foliage cover, and heavy rainfall produces a self-regulating system with air temperatures at ground level remaining remarkably steady day and night, summer and winter, at 26°C to 30°C (79°F to 86°F).

Tortoises first evolved in this type of climate, and those native to these areas, such as *Geochelone carbonaria* (the Red-footed Tortoise) from South America, do not appear to have any temperature control system but rely on the forest to keep them at the correct temperature. Keeping such a tortoise anywhere other than in a rainforest climate obviously requires housing where the air temperature is thermostatically controlled day and night, summer and winter, at about 28°C (82°F).

Equatorial Island Tortoises

The tortoises in the Galapagos and the Seychelles live in areas where the air temperatures are generally 26°C (79°F) to 30°C (86°F) but occasionally rise to 50°C (122°F). The tortoises have developed procedures to reduce their body temperatures below the air temperature in these extreme conditions. In these circumstances they avoid direct sunlight and wallow in muddy pools, then allow the water to evaporate from their bodies, producing a cooling effect. For obvious reasons, these conditions must be duplicated to provide a suitable thermal environment for these animals outside their natural habitat.

Desert Tortoises

Some species of tortoises, such as the Desert Tortoise *(Gopherus agassizi)* of North America, live in hot deserts. Deserts are places of extreme temperatures. However, 6 to 9 inches (15 to 22.5 cm) below the soil surface the extremes are evened out because of the thermal insulation of the soil. These tortoises dig burrows and only venture out when the temperatures are acceptable to them.

Mediterranean (Hibernating) Tortoises

These tortoises live in areas north and south of the equatorial regions where, in general, the air temperature alone is insufficiently high to raise their body temperatures to the preferred 30°C (86°F). They have developed three methods of coping with the problem. During the summer days they use the radiant heat from the sun to raise their body temperature above the air temperature. During summer nights they bury themselves to retain as much heat as possible. In the winter, when the air temperature becomes low and the hours of sunshine diminish, these methods prove inadequate. These tortoises have therefore developed a strategy of hibernation to get around this temporary problem.

It is the functioning of this fourth group of animals that this book sets out to explore. Most of my trials and experiments have been carried out with Spur-thighed Greek Tortoises, *Testudo graeca*, but, provided common sense is used, much of this work gives a better understanding of the husbandry of all Mediterranean tortoises.

BASKING

Every tortoise owner has noticed that, when the sun shines, Mediterranean tortoises in an English garden find a spot in a shaft of sunlight and aim their carapaces at the sun. Provided they are not frightened or disturbed, they remain like that until they are warm to the touch. Then, and only then, do they wander off to find food. What is not so obvious is what is actually happening.

The surface colours of the carapace are colours that absorb rather than reflect infra-red radiation. Also, the surface is covered with minute pores into which the radiation shines but cannot escape. This raises the temperature of the carapace.

The blood circulatory system of tortoises is different from that of mammals. In mammals the blood flow is directed to the lungs and then to the main muscle groups and organs. In tortoises, a large proportion of the flow is directed across the back of the body, under the carapace, to collect the warmth and distribute it around the body.

In the Mediterranean areas where these animals are native, the summer air temperatures are somewhat warmer than in Britain, but, much more significantly, the average sunshine per year is between 2,500 and 3,500 hours. In Britain, the average is 1,500 hours per year. Not only that, but the sun is at a lower angle in the sky. This means that a tortoise in a British garden, which has only about one-third of the radiant energy available for body heating that would be available to it in its natural range, can utilise food at a much reduced rate. It therefore eats less, grows less, is less active, and its immune system is less effective. It is essential, if Mediterranean tortoises are to be kept well and healthy for extended periods, that extra basking facilities are provided for those summer days when the sunshine falls short of Mediterranean standards.

I have carried out a series of trials to try to find out as much as I could about basking behaviour—with interesting results.

First, the state of health of the tortoise is significant. If a reflector lamp is shining vertically down onto the floor, the temperature under it can be measured. It is hottest under the centre, and the temperature drops off concentrically until it reaches air temperature. A healthy, active tortoise will go to the hottest available spot, remain there until it attains its required body temperature, then will go off to eat, explore, or whatever. A sick tortoise normally will choose a spot between the cold edge and hot centre where the temperature is about 30°C (86°F), and there it will remain without moving. A very sick tortoise with a potentially terminal problem will totally avoid any warmth and will attempt to hibernate instead.

There is a difference between basking behaviour of males and females. Females tend to bask for extended periods, but males tend to be restless and bask for a series of shorter periods. There also is a change in basking behaviour with anorexic tortoises.

I have provided alternative types of basking facilities in order to see which the tortoises prefer. I found that if only one type of facility is provided, the tortoises will use it, whether it is white lamp, coloured lamp, infra-red emitter, heat pad, central heating radiator, or coal fire. If, however, alternatives are offered, then the tortoises use the lamps that provide a parallel downward beam of white light in preference to others, even, strangely enough, in preference to sources such as infra-red emitters that ought, theoretically, to be more efficient for basking purposes. The conclusion I reached from this was that tortoises recognised appropriate basking sites in the wild primarily by spotting shafts of sunlight and adjusting their position within that site by feeling the warmth on their backs. One interesting observation is that tortoises kept in greenhouses or conservatories do appear to have problems. Inside a greenhouse, temperatures generally are warmer than outside in a garden, an obvious advantage. However, there are two counterbalancing disadvantages. First, the tortoise tries to maintain a steady temperature, but temperatures under glass fluctuate widely when the sun shines or stops shining. Second, the tortoise appears to have problems in finding sensible places to bask under glass, presumably because the light is scattered by the glass. The only time a tortoise appears to demonstrate "normal" basking behaviour under glass is when, for instance, a tree overhangs the greenhouse and its leaves break the light up into distinct beams.

Ambient air temperature has a bearing on basking. I have tried keeping tortoises with constant basking facilities and varying air temperatures. As might be expected, the lower the air temperature the more time tortoises spent basking.

If used in conjunction with a basking temperature of 35°C (95°F), the acceptable range of air temperature for healthy tortoises appears to be 15°C (59°F) to 25°C (77°F). At the lower end of the range, the tortoises are disinclined to get out of bed in the morning, and when they do get up they spend most of their time basking and their appetites are poor. As the temperature rises, their appetites improve. As the air temperature approaches 30°C (86°F) the tortoises start to favour cooler, shadier spots, and bask only for very short periods.

Basking lamps, when used as described, effectively replace the Mediterranean sunshine. Tortoises react to the lamps as they would react to the sun. They get up when the lamps are switched on, and go to bed when they are switched off. Both the breeding cycle and the hibernation cycle are annual, and there are indications that day length has an effect on these cycles.

Although many acceptable setups are possible, I have found that for keeping healthy *Testudo graeca, hermanni,* and *marginata* during the summer, the following setup has given me the best results:

1) A daytime ambient air temperature between 20°C and 25°C (68°F to 77°F). Very sick tortoises need air temperatures of 25°C to 28°C (77°F to 82°F).

2) A nighttime air temperature between 10°C and 15°C (50°F to 59°F).

3) A "nest" area for overnight where the tortoise can bury itself in insulating material such as straw, leaves, or shredded paper.

4) Vertically hung, uncoloured tungsten filament spot lamps with their height above the ground adjusted to give a temperature on the ground of 35°C (95°F). (I use 100 watt 30° angle R95 reflector bulbs.) Sufficient bulbs need to be used to create a warm area large enough for all tortoises to bask comfortably.

5) The lamps are switched on and off with a timer that is adjusted monthly so that the day length corresponds to Mediterranean daylight areas:

April 1—12 hours 0 minutes
May 1—13 hours 20 minutes
June 1—14 hours 20 minutes
July 1—14 hours 40 minutes
August 1—14 hours 20 minutes
September 1—13 hours 20 minutes
October 1—12 hours 0 minutes.

The average sunshine hours per year where wild Mediterranean tortoises live is 3,000. The equivalent in Britain using no lamps is 1,500 hours (i.e., much too low). The equivalent artificial sunshine hours using lamps to the full amount of the foregoing table is 4,400 hours per year (i.e., much too high). The hobbyist of course must remember that in nature rainy or cloudy days affect the amount of sunlight available and prevent it from reaching theoretical levels.

When too little radiant heat is used, tortoises are less active, grow less, have problems recovering from disease, and wounds are very slow to heal.

When too much radiant heat is used, tortoises can grow more rapidly than normal, leading to abnormal development. There are no differences whatsoever in the requirements of adults, juveniles, or hatchlings. Most owners are inclined to keep adults too cold and hatchlings too hot. I recommend that basking lamps be provided with a timer set to give the hours in the foregoing table, but that the lamps be turned off from time to time to simulate cloudy days in the Mediterranean. Be guided by activity levels, growth rates, appetite, and general health.

6) Because large indoor areas are, in general, ruled out on grounds of cost, and because tortoise behaviour is greatly modified when confined in small areas, access to outdoor areas in addition to the indoor area is recommended.

7) Tortoises should be housed in separate areas, either singly or in small groups.

In order to achieve maximum visibility of the animals, zoos generally prefer to use underfloor heating pads to obtain the 35°C (95°F) basking temperature. Theoretically this should work, but in practice it is difficult to get them to act fully natural by this method. In particular, tortoises kept this way tend to dig in above the heaters at night rather than find a separate nest to sleep in.

CLEANLINESS

If a tortoise is dirty, the efficiency of its heat exchange mechanism is reduced. This is obviously undesirable. Putting oil on tortoises is worse. The oil fills the pores, attracts dirt, and makes cleaning difficult. Oil and dirt also make shell rot more likely. I do know that many previously written books recommend oiling, but they are wrong!

Wash tortoises regularly with soap and water using a fingernail brush or a toothbrush. If oil has been used, it is necessary to scrub the carapace using dish detergent many times in order to remove it from the pores. Protect the tortoise's eyes with a towel when washing. Tortoises are much prettier when they are clean.

Tortoises must be kept reasonably clean. Dirt or oil clogging the tortoise's pores affect the efficiency of the heat exchange system within the tortoise's body. Use soap or detergent and water, with a soft brush. Protect the tortoise's eyes. Photo by Susan C. Miller.

HIBERNATION

In their natural environment, as winter approaches, Mediterranean tortoises try to hold their body temperatures at 30°C (86°F) for as long as possible. However, as the day length shortens, the sun retreats to a lower angle in the sky, and the air temperature falls, it gets more and more difficult. Eventually the tortoises give up the struggle and search out cool shady areas rather than warm sunny ones. This causes the body temperature to fall dramatically (to 10 to 15°C [50 to 59°F]) and in turn causes loss of appetite. For about four weeks the tortoises do not eat but continue to defecate and urinate. By the end of this period the tortoises have empty guts and are ready to hibernate.

The soil in the areas where the tortoises live is, in general, light, well-drained, and has a high limestone content. Soil of this nature has very low thermal conductivity. During the winter the soil surface temperature is approximately the same as the air temperature (approximately 0°C [32°F]), but just a few inches below the surface it is at the average of summer and winter temperature (approximately 15°C [59°F]). This creates a temperature gradient that the tortoises use.

Just as the correct body temperature is important during the summer, so it is during hibernation, except that the tortoises now attempt to achieve a body temperature of 4 to 5°C (39 to 41°F). They do this by digging down until they find the right temperature. Please note— tortoises appear to dig to where the temperature is correct rather than to any particular depth.

When the tortoise's body temperature is 30°C (86°F) it operates its metabolism on "open cycle": it eats food and passes out faeces, water, and uric acid compounds. When the tortoise's body is at 4°C (39°F) it operates its metabolism on "closed cycle": it consumes stored body fats and stores waste products in the kidneys. At this temperature the tortoise remains inactive, its heartbeat and breathing slowing to a tiny fraction of their summer values. In this state the tortoise uses very little energy and can exist passively for extended periods. The body tissues consumed, and hence the waste products stored, can be checked by weighing before and after hibernation, and if necessary, at intervals during hibernation.

Note: If tortoises are weighed during hibernation, don't bring them into a warm room to do it. Weigh them where the air temperature is 4 to 5°C (39-41°F) to avoid disturbing their rest.

When I carried out tests I found that *provided:*

1) the tortoise has an empty gut when hibernation starts;

2) the tortoise's body temperature remains at 4°C (39°F) *at all times*; and

3) the tortoise weighs more than 1,500 gms (52.5 oz)

—the weight loss over a four-month period generally is less than 5 gms (0.18 oz). The exact loss is beyond the capabilities of my experimental apparatus to determine. There are problems due, firstly, to accuracy of weighing; secondly, to the weight of condensation that sometimes occurs on the tortoise during hibernation; and thirdly, to the difficulty of keeping temperatures accurate over extended periods. However, my figures indicate a weight loss of about 0.1% per month for healthy tortoises kept accurately at 4°C (39°F).

In order to get some idea of the time that it is possible to hibernate tortoises, I allowed a healthy 10-week-old tortoise to lose over 23 % of her body weight over a 15-week hibernation. She started eating within two days of waking up, steadily regained her lost weight, and showed no apparent ill effects from her ordeal. If one combines these figures with those quoted in the previous paragraph, the maximum length of time that it should be possible to hibernate a tortoise is

$$\frac{23.5}{0.1} \times \frac{1}{12} = 19.5 \text{ years!!}$$

I am not, of course, recommending that you should try to hibernate tortoises for anything approaching this length of time! The method of arriving at the figure is basically extrapolation, which is notoriously unreliable. However, it does show that for successful hibernation it is temperature that is the critical factor, and the length of the hibernation is relatively unimportant.

If a tortoise hibernates in a temperature-controlled box and a careful check is kept of the animal's body temperature, several interesting facts will be observed. At 4 to 5°C (39 to 41°F), the tortoise remains totally inactive. If the temperature falls, the tortoise digs downward by scraping with its front claws and pushing with its back legs. If the temperature rises above 4 to 5°C (39 to 41°F), the tortoise digs upward by the same method. These appear to be reflexive rather than conscious actions. The tortoise appears to remain asleep while digging unless digging is prolonged. Given the naturally occurring temperature gradient in the soil in its home environment, these actions form an automatic system for maintaining an accurate, low body temperature.

By comparing hibernation weight loss with hibernation temperature, there appears to be a direct relationship where time spent at temperatures above 6°C (43°F) or below 3°C (38°F) is proportional to the time spent digging, which is in turn proportional to weight loss, which is in turn proportional to the waste products stored in the kidneys, and which is in turn related to blood urea levels.

For smaller tortoises and juveniles, the temperature range to show these effects appears smaller. Again my experimental procedures were only capable of qualitative results and conclusions. There is considerable room for quantitative experiments.

If the tortoise's body temperature rises to 8 to 10°C (46 to 50°F), the tortoise wakes and digs to the surface. The exact temperature at which these various things happen appears to be an individual characteristic of each tortoise. However, the general pattern is always the same and there appears to be a tendency for smaller tortoises to waken at lower temperatures than larger tortoises.

If the tortoise's temperature is allowed to fall too low, damage will occur. Initially eye damage is caused, possibly by freezing of the moisture in and on the eye, possibly by other mechanisms. The lower the temperature the more extensive the damage, eventually causing death. For obvious reasons, I have not carried out experiments to find at exactly what temperatures these problems occur, but I would suggest that no tortoise be kept in conditions that allow its body temperature to fall below 2°C (36°F).

DISEASE PROBLEMS WHILE HIBERNATING

In general, diseases are caused by organisms living within the tortoise's body. These organisms can be affected by medication, the tortoise's immune system, and the tortoise's body temperature.

Active, warm, well-nourished tortoises have effective immune systems that cope well with minor problems. During hibernation the immune system is less effective, hence tortoises hibernated with major disease problems will get worse and may die. To balance this effect, at 4°C (39°F) most disease organisms cease to grow and multiply, which is why refrigerators keep food fresh. This means that if a tortoise is hibernated while suffering from a minor problem the disease progresses, but at a much reduced rate. It should be realized, however, that diseases can progress at a much higher rate at 7°C (45°F) than they can at 4°C(39°F), hence, accurate temperature control is vital.

Although putting a tortoise into hibernation with mild disease problems is not normally fatal, it is much better to keep a constant check on possible diseases during the summer and treat any problems if and when they occur. Do not delay treatment until death is imminent. If a course of treatment extends into the period that the tortoise would normally hibernate, hibernation should be delayed by keeping air temperature, light levels, day length, and basking facilities at summer levels until it is cured. The tortoise then should be allowed to empty its gut for three or four weeks and then hibernated. Do not avoid hibernation altogether, because doing this can add anorexia and kidney damage to the tortoise's existing problems. Lack of hibernation also can produce long-term behavioural and sexual problems.

RECOMMENDED HIBERNATION PROCEDURES

Method 1

Leave the tortoise out of doors to "run down" and then to dig in and hibernate naturally. Given large areas with plenty of choice, the tortoise will choose a cold, dry place with loose soil and evergreen shrub cover. An ideal situation is in a corner of a garden that is permanently in shadow, with light, dry, limey soil, sheltered by ornamental conifers. (These trees produce an effective rain cover in the winter but have weak root systems that a tortoise normally can dig through. The leaf litter under these trees also is effective insulation.)

There is an instinctive human reasoning that one is not doing one's best for the tortoise to leave it outside in the winter. However, provided that the conditions are as described, this is a very good method. Of all the tortoises that I have seen suffering from post-hibernation problems, more than 99% have been hibernated using "box and insulation" methods and less than 1% have been hibernated out of doors.

One potential problem that owners sometimes ask about is attack by wild animals. In the outdoor area that I have used to hibernate tortoises, there are foxes, rats, mice, magpies, crows, pigeons, squirrels, feral cats, jays, and stray dogs, none of which has ever interfered with the tortoises in any way whatsoever during hibernation or at any other time. (Occasionally, dogs will attack tortoises during the summer, thus I do not think it is a good idea to keep both dogs and tortoises.)

Another potential problem that owners worry about is frost damage. If a tortoise is buried 6 inches (15 cm) down in *dry* soil it will come to no harm even with short periods at temperatures well below freezing. The major problem is dampness. Wet soil conducts heat about 100 times more effectively than dry soil, hence a tortoise buried in damp soil is in danger if the temperature falls even a little below freezing.

Method 2

Sometimes a tortoise will attempt to dig in an unsatisfactory place, such as above rocks or large tree roots where it cannot dig deeply enough. If it is only half buried, cover the tortoise with leaf litter or similar material. Leave it for a few days until it is well asleep. Dig a new hole in a cold dry place and re-bury the sleeping tortoise. This must be done in the cool of the evening rather than the warmth of the day to avoid disturbing the tortoise. There should be 4 to 6 inches (10 to 15 cm) of loose soil both above and below the tortoise so it can dig up or down. Keep the area dry by surrounding it with a ring of bricks, fill the space with straw or leaves, then a layer of soil, then cover the lot with slates or a plastic sheet to keep the rain off.

Method 3

Bury a plastic dustbin full of peat in the ground in a shady place. Cover it with a roof, preferably not transparent, to keep the rain off. At the appropriate moment (as described in Method 2) bury the tortoise in the peat. This method is an improvement on Methods 1 and 2, because one can be reasonably sure the peat will remain dry, plus it is cheap and relatively easy. It uses the tortoise's natural instincts, and it is possible to control hibernation conditions more accurately.

One possible problem is flooding. If this happens, clear everything out promptly and start again.

Another possible problem is winter temperatures that are *too high*. The temperature of the tortoise can be checked either with an electronic thermometer with its sensor taped on the tortoise's carapace or with a normal thermometer pushed to an appropriate depth in the peat. If temperatures are too high, the surface of the peat can be chilled by putting a plastic container on the surface and filling it with ice cubes. These would obviously need to be replaced as they melted. This is effective and mimics conditions in the wild, but obviously can be time consuming if a warm spell is prolonged.

Method 4

Put the tortoise in a box of insulating material in a shed or garage. This is the basic method that most people use, and it is the method I have used to obtain most of my experimental data. It is, however, a method full of potential pitfalls, and *great care* needs to be exercised if one decides to use this method.

A single box is not sufficient. If the air temperature falls the tortoise will dig down to the bottom of the box. It is then sitting on a cold floor and frost damage is almost inevitable. The box should be double with *at least* 4 inches (10 cm) of good quality insulation between the boxes, and straw, shredded paper, or polystyrene chips (not beads) in the inner box. This means that the outer box needs to be *at least* tea chest size for a medium-sized tortoise. This will not keep the tortoise warm or cold, but it will even out the day and night fluctuations of temperature, though not longer term changes.

Using this method means that the tortoise can no longer use its instincts to achieve its correct hibernating temperature. It is, therefore, essential that the owner does the job instead. The tortoise should be kept as accurately as possible at 4 to 5°C (39 to 41°F). This temperature can be checked by using either a remote electronic thermometer with a probe taped to the tortoise's carapace or a maximum-minimum thermometer to daily check the day and night temperatures in the room surrounding the box. The average of these temperatures will give the tortoise's body temperature.

If the temperature is wrong, there are several ways of correcting it. First, one can move the box to a different place where the air temperature is correct. Second, one can, provided the area is thermally very well insulated, open windows during the day and close them at night to raise the temperature a few degrees. Conversely, open the windows at night and close them during the day to lower the temperature a few degrees. If these manoeuvres prove insufficient, a heater can be used for a few minutes a day to raise the room temperature during an extended cold spell, or ice packs can be placed in the insulation between inner and outer boxes during a warm spell. If the ice pack method is used it is necessary to use the electronic thermometer—a maximum-minimum thermometer will no longer give the right answer.

Method 5

The London Zoo uses a constantly monitored refrigerated room to over-winter those reptiles that require low, constant winter temperatures. It is feasible to use refrigeration equipment to provide constant accurate conditions on a domestic scale.

After the "run down" period, put the tortoise in a box containing shredded newspaper or similar material and put the box in a suitably prepared fridge, allowing room for air circulation around the box. Beware of two potential problems. Domestic fridges are hermetically sealed. Although hibernating tortoises need very little air, they do need some. Don't suffocate them! Remove a small section of the door seal to allow air to enter and leave the fridge. Because cold air sinks below warm air, a normal fridge is warm at the top and cold at the bottom. This is the reverse of the soil temperature gradient that the tortoise's instincts have evolved to cope with. Carefully check the operating temperatures in several places inside the fridge to ensure that this effect is not significantly large and also that the thermostat keeps the fridge consistently at 4 to 5°C (39 to 41°F).

Some soft drink companies supply fridges for the storage, display, and retail sale of chilled soft drinks. These fridges have strong adjustable shelves that will accommodate all sizes of tortoises. They have forced air circulation that keeps the whole of the interior at an even temperature, and they have double glazed doors so that tortoises and thermometers can be observed without opening the door. They are ideal for the purposes of hibernation.

Although this method obviously is more expensive and more time-consuming to set up than the other methods described, it is potentially the best. Once a fridge is set up, it is easy, the results are superb, and one can organize the hibernation timing to suit various priorities.

CHECKING

Whichever hibernation method is used, it is straightforward to check how successful one has been by weighing the tortoise immediately after hibernation. The smaller the weight loss, the better you have done.

HIBERNATING HATCHLINGS

Owners frequently show great reluctance to hibernate hatchlings because they appear to be so small and fragile. However, tortoises in the wild hatch between mid-summer and late autumn and hibernate for three or four months for their first winter. Unhibernated hatchlings tend to grow faster than normal, so carapace and other deformities are more common because normal annular scute growth is not possible.

I have always hibernated hatchlings. However, their small size means that they are much more susceptible to body temperature changes, hence subsequent water loss and related problems. Extreme care should be taken to see that the hibernation temperature is as accurate and steady as possible. Checks on weight loss should be made at regular intervals. Weighing should be done when the air temperature is 4 to 5°C (39-41°F) to avoid waking the tortoises. If the weight loss exceeds 10%, I would recommend awakening the hatchling and bringing it into summer conditions.

WAKING FROM HIBERNATION

In the wild, because the change from winter to summer is so rapid, the air and sun temperatures are sufficient to enable the tortoise to get its body to 30°C (86°F) immediately on waking from hibernation. This enables the tortoise to eat immediately and to clear its kidneys of waste products built up over hibernation. In northern climes, condition frequently are inadequate at this time of the year. It is important that one provide sufficient air temperatures and basking facilities after waking. This is in contrast to the correct procedures for cooling when going into hibernation, where a steady change is better.

There are some owners who feel that provided a tortoise is kept well during the summer, the hibernation techniques described in this chapter are unnecessary. This is not so. Both no hibernation and inadequate hibernation are potentially lethal in the long run.

AVOIDING HIBERNATION

If a Mediterranean tortoise is kept over the winter period in artificial summer conditions (i.e., air temperature approximately 20°C (68°F), basking spot temperature approximately 35°C (95°F), day length approximately 14 hours, and high daytime light levels) it will not hibernate. Not hibernating creates no short-term problems, but can create a multiplicity of long-term problems. With adults it can cause anorexia and kidney problems, and with hatchlings it can cause dietary problems. It also affects the tortoise's "body clock," sometimes producing inappropriate instinctive behaviour, plus it affects breeding performance.

Avoiding hibernation can be a useful trick to gain time for treating potentially lethal diseases, but it should be regarded as an emergency treatment and should not be done as a matter of course. If medical treatment or recuperation from medical treatment extending into the winter months is necessary, it is generally much better to delay hibernation than to avoid it totally.

DIET

Dietary recommendations for *Testudo graeca* have undergone a steady evolution over the past ten years. The recommendations made in this chapter are subtly different from those I was making merely 18 months ago. This is because of the steady progress of understanding in this area. The pioneer in this field was Don Reid, who, with a variety of dietary experiments on hatchlings at the Cotswold Wildlife Park, showed that many of the previously mysterious syndromes that afflicted hatchling tortoises were in fact caused by dietary deficiencies. Andy Highfield of the Tortoise Trust has published a comprehensive compilation of the results of most of the research work done in this field.

This work, combined with my own research, enables me to at last make predictions of the consequences of various dietary regimes with a degree of confidence not previously felt.

In my tests I have found no difference whatever between the optimum dietary requirements of new hatchlings and large adults (except, of course, quantity). There is, however, a difference between the two in the effects of an incorrect diet. If a tortoise spends ten years on an optimal diet, e.g., in the wild, and then is fed a poor diet, e.g., after importation to northern Europe, the resulting problems are very slow to take effect. Typically it takes 5 to 20 years to show unmistakable deficiency effects. This is partly a real effect and partly a failure of diagnosis.

Hatchlings are different. They generally will show symptoms within two to three weeks if the diet is inadequate, and death normally will occur between one and 36 months from hatching. The reason for the difference is that inadequate diets normally result in abnormal carapace and bone development. An imported tortoise has a basic existing bone structure, but a hatchling does not. If any reader is contemplating research in this field I would strongly recommend using hatchlings—you might otherwise be dead before you get any results!

The areas that most *Testudo graeca*

inhabit are basically sparsely vegetated infertile upland areas. The tortoises are opportunist feeders and will eat a wide variety of plant material, leaves, flowers, and fruit as available and in season. This mode of feeding gives the tortoises the wide range of vitamins and trace elements that they need.

Tortoises normally do not eat a plant in the wild, but instead eat a flower or the most succulent leaves and then move on. They also tend to defecate and urinate as they eat. This has considerable survival value in sparsely vegetated areas. They tend not to destroy their food plants, but instead fertilise and water them before moving on. However, having the same instincts in captivity means that the tortoises tend to walk forward over a pile of food provided by human hands and then urinate or defecate on it. This means that internal parasites are very common among captive animals and good hygiene is not easy.

DIETARY RECOMMENDATIONS

The basic diet should consist of low-protein, high-fibre food with high mineral and vitamin content together with a large proportion of calcium carbonate. Following are detailed suggestions for achieving this.

Wild Plants

The major part of the diet should consist of a varying selection of any wild-growing weeds, leaves, and flowers, as seasonally available, that will be taken by the tortoise. Three plants that tortoises eat in the wild that also grow widely in northern Europe are dandelions, sow thistle, and clover. My experience is that tortoises will not eat plants that are poisonous to them, so one can afford to try different plants for a change of diet with negligible risk of harming the tortoise. Dandelions grow best on very impoverished soil, clover grows best on rich soil.

Cultivated Vegetables

In addition to wild plants, one can feed

virtually any green vegetables that are commonly used for human consumption, i.e., cabbage, spinach, cress, water cress, broccoli, cauliflower, beans, peas, sprouting seeds, etc. One must bear in mind, however, that a tortoise's digestion works better on low protein, high fibre foods, and in general, cultivated plants contain higher levels of protein and lower levels of fibre than wild plants. Early and late in the season, when wild plants are not abundant, vegetables make an acceptable alternative to wild plants and are a useful dietary addition at all times.

Grass

Mediterranean tortoises do not appear to be able to digest the cellulose that is a major constitutent of grasses. However, while eating some plants, such as clover, tortoises often take adjacent grass, and there is evidence to show that this, while not providing any nourishment, aids the digestive process by providing bulk and fibre.

Vitamins and Minerals

The food taken in the wild generally is higher in vitamins and trace elements than any foods normally available in northern Europe. Tortoises can live for a very long time and minor deficiency problems can show effects over long periods. Hence it is recommended that a small quantity of vitamin/mineral supplement be added to the food on a regular basis. Although any supplement is helpful, one containing as many constitutents as possible appears best. Several excellent vitamin/mineral supplements blended specifically for reptiles are available through your local pet shop.

Salad Items

Lettuces, cucumbers, and tomatoes are hybrid plants developed for human use. These plants have been developed to look good, taste nice, and grow quickly. This makes them cheap and also ensures that they contain very little useful food value—ideal for overfed European mankind, but not ideal for tortoises. Because they look, smell, and taste good, they are readily taken by tortoises and hence are useful for making other foods attractive and palatable, but they should not form the majority of the diet.

Milk Products

Milk is produced by mammals to nourish their young. Reptiles such as tortoises do not produce milk and their bodies do not possess the mechanisms for using milk and its products, such as butter, cheese, and yogurt. There is growing evidence to suggest that feeding tortoises milk products for extended periods leads to potentially lethal liver damage.

Manufactured Foods

The evidence here is very thin, but my instinct leads me to suggest that bread, cake, jam, and similar items are very unlikely to be advantageous dietary items. It is recommended that anything containing sugar or salt additives be avoided.

Meat

Meat is very high in protein. Some tortoises will eat meat in the form of cat or dog food. If they are fed this unnatural diet it may lead to some short-term problems and definitely will lead to major long-term problems if fed regularly. The increased protein in the stomach causes a much-increased population of intestinal organisms. This may lead to gastroenteritis or internal parasite problems. For normal growth, particularly of carapace and bone, the correct ratio of protein to calcium is important. If meat is used in the diet it becomes impossible to get this ratio correct. This leads in turn to osteodystrophy (i.e., progressive weakening of bones, etc.) and/or abnormal carapace development. Regular high protein intake also causes long-term liver damage that is lethal.

Calcium

The areas in the wild where *Testudo graeca* lives are extremely rich in calcium compared with most areas in northern Europe. The Atlas Mountains in Morocco are limestone (calcium carbonate) thousands of feet thick. Similarly, the areas in

Israel, Syria, Turkey, Iran, and Algeria where the tortoises live are either limestone hills or internal drainage basins where water carrying dissolved calcium from the hills evaporates to leave the soil rich in calcium deposits. The plants growing in these areas are rich in calcium. Also, the tortoises eat small pieces of limestone that they find lying about.

The hard parts of a tortoise's body (i.e., carapace, plastron, scales, claws, external mouth parts, and skeleton) are constructed of calcium compounds, mainly calcium phosphate. These comprise about one-third of the total weight of the animal. Human beings obtain most of their calcium from milk and meat products—sources not available to tortoises. Tortoises use calcium carbonate (from limestone) plus phosphorus (from green leaves) plus vitamin D (from leaves and vitamin supplements or internally manufactured using the ultra-violet rays from sunlight) to manufacture calcium phosphate. If any of these ingredients are in short supply, the tortoise will suffer from osteodystrophy, particularly if simultaneously eating a high protein diet. In imported adults, the symptoms of this problem are:

1) Claws are curved or bent rather than straight.

2) Growth areas around each scute are undercut.

3) Accidental mechanical damage to carapace, claws, or plastron fails to heal.

4) If the tortoise is kept at adequate temperatures and on an otherwise adequate diet, obesity develops around the shoulders and hips.

5) Biting the hard calacium carbonate keeps the edges of the mouth in shape. Hence, a shortage of calcium in the diet normally is accompanied by an overgrown top beak. The hinged rear portion of the plastron, particularly in females, is a device to facilitate egglaying, not a sign of osteodystrophy.

In hatchlings, the problems arising from osteodystrophy are more severe because the animal does not have a hard preformed skeleton on which to rely. In hatchlings:

1) The carapace and plastron fail to harden adequately.

2) Carapace scutes grow in a pyramidal fashion rather than evenly rounded.

3) The edges of the mouth fail to harden and the tortoise then can only eat softer foods, which in turn leads to steadily worsening dietary problems and hence to malnutrition and death. This process takes one to 18 months.

4) If the hatchling survives this malnutrition phase but continues to receive a low-calcium diet, the carapace becomes hollow within the pyramids. This takes up the space that normally would be occupied by the lungs, and the animal's breathing becomes steadily more difficult. Death frequently will then be triggered by what would otherwise be a minor respiratory problem.

Osteodystrophy is, at the time of writing, the cause of the majority of hatchling deaths. (The majority of adult tortoise deaths are caused by a lack of understanding of the tortoise's temperature control problems.)

Captive tortoises should be fed calcium carbonate as an integral part of their diet. The quantities required are generally much larger than most owners seem to realise. It is not a medicine, it is a food. It is the raw material from which the tortoise builds the hard parts of its body. I have carried out tests to find maximum and minimum amounts that should be fed. Feeding too little has far-reaching, long-term, potentially lethal effects. Feeding too much appears to have only minor effects. Feeding quantities equal to the weight of all other food consumed appears to show no ill effects. If quantities greater than the digestive system can handle are fed, the tortoise becomes constipated, but this passes as soon as quantities are reduced.

Watch the amount and shape of new carapace growth carefully to see that it corresponds to normal growth in the wild. If it does, you have your quantities right. **Start by adding about 10% by weight to the diet.**

The easiest source of calcium carbonate to use is clean, crushed egg shells sprinkled over the food. To human tastes this seems to spoil a tasty salad, but the tortoises seem to enjoy it. An alternative is to use cuttlebone powdered with a cheese grater. Cuttlebone has a problem, because it smells of fish! This smell is alien to an inland dwelling tortoise, and some are put off by it. The smell can be removed by soaking and drying several times or by leaving the cuttlebone outside in the rain for a few weeks. In addition to putting calcium on the food, I normally leave raw cuttlebone or piles of ground egg shells around, available to the tortoise if they want extra.

Another good possible source is "limestone flour." This is clean, crushed limestone (calcium carbonate). It is used in the food industry to make bread white and it can be obtained from quarrying companies, though normal minimum quantities are 25 kg (55-pound) sacks.

I have tried using sterilised powdered bone meal (calcium phosphate), but have found that although the tortoises take it readily, they develop ravenous thirsts and do not grow naturally. This is presumably due to excess phosphorus in their systems.

I know that some people have used calcium preparations sold for human consumption. This normally is in the form of calcium lactate, which is manufactured from powdered milk. Because of the known long-term risks from milk products, I have steered clear of using this, but I have no proof of either advantages or problems arising from using this form of calcium.

Drink

Humans need to constantly replace water lost by perspiration and urination, hence they need to drink. Tortoises are adapted to live in areas with little exposed water. Healthy tortoises DO NOT drink. Tortoises do not perspire. Also, their kidneys split up what humans pass as urine into virtually clear water and a white creamy substance that contains compounds of uric acid. They only pass out the water when it is surplus to requirements. They can obtain all the water they need from the food they eat, even if the plants they eat appear to be dried up.

Occasionally, tortoises drink copiously in order to flush unwanted chemicals from their kidneys. This happens, for instance, if injections of antibiotics are given and the antibiotics build up in the kidneys. It also happens when urates build up in the kidneys due to incorrect thermal husbandry.

Under either of these circumstances water should be offered. Make sure the tortoise is warm, then stand it in a bowl of clean lukewarm water and let the tortoise stay there for 5 to 10 minutes. Offering a saucer of water usually does not work, it just gets spilled. Weigh the tortoise before and after, and the weight difference will tell you how much the tortoise has drunk. When tortoises drink they do not pause for breath, but drink continuously until sated.

Testudo graeca (left) and *Geochelone pardalis* feeding on a lettuce leaf. The leaf is thoroughly moistened and glistens with drops of water. Tortoises do NOT normally require more water than is naturally in their food. Photo by Isabelle Francais courtesy of *Parrots of the World.*

SENSES

There are considerable misconceptions about the ways that animals in general, and tortoises in particular, make sense of the world and how they interact with each other. Owners tend to assume that their pets sense the world in the same way as humans and react with human instincts. It is not difficult to show that these assumptions are often wide of the mark. Any tortoise owner can check most of the statements made in this chapter, but it is important to realise that a warm and healthy tortoise's reactions tend to be quick and positive. Cold or sick tortoises become lethargic and their reactions slow, sometimes to the point of non-existence.

Hearing

Tortoises have ears situated on either side of their heads, to the rear of their eyes. If you stand behind a screen so that you cannot be seen and downwind so that you cannot be smelled, you can make a considerable noise and a tortoise will not react in any way. They appear to be virtually deaf. Many owners tell me "My tortoise comes when I call." Yes, some will, but they are using smell and sight, not hearing. Try going through the motions of "calling without making any noise" (i.e., using only body language...hand motions, etc.) and you should find that the tortoise comes just the same! Some experiments have re-ported that tortoises can hear very low frequency sounds. They do appear to be able to detect footsteps, but it is not clear if they use hearing, touch, or balance to achieve this.

Balance

This sense is important to the tortoise, not only for the obvious reasons of enabling the tortoise to walk efficiently, but also to enable the tortoise to dig in the right direction when hibernating, when other senses are of little assistance. Hold a tortoise so it faces you and tilt its body slowly from side to side. The tortoise will twist its head, trying to keep it in a horizontal position. Watching a tortoise climb over rocks or on steep slopes allows one to observe the use of both side to side and fore and aft balance.

Sight

There are significant differences between human eyesight and tortoise eyesight. In humans, eyesight is the primary sense. In tortoises, eyesight is important but its main functions are as an early warning system and as an adjunct to the primary sense of smell. The eyes are set in the side of the head giving about 300 degrees of all around vision compared with about 160 degree for humans. This means that it is almost impossible to approach a tortoise from any direction without being spotted. It also means that forward binocular vision is worse than in humans. Many owners observe that tortoises often have difficulty judging the exact position of food, par-ticularly if it is closer than about an inch from the nostrils.

Compared with human eyes, tortoise eyes are very sensitive to movement but are poor at sorting out colour and detail. If one stands motionless one becomes part of the general background and become virtually invisible to the tortoise.

Smell

A tortoise's sense of smell is infinitely more acute than a human's. It is difficult for a human to imagine what this means. The human world is built up of visual images. The tortoise's world is built of "smell" images. We do not even have the right words to cope with the concept! When a tortoise is startled by a movement in its field of vision, it "freezes." It stretches out its front legs to raise the front of its body as high as possible, stretches out its neck, and lifts its head as high as possible. Then, with its nostrils in this elevated position, the tortoise palpates its throat to rapidly draw air in and out over the nasal sense organs. This gives the tortoise a "picture" of his surroundings. When the tortoise is cold or sick, and hence slower in its reaction speed, many owners construe the tortoise's slow attempts to assume this position as a desire to be petted, and then his subsequent slow withdrawal from this position as an appreciation of the petting. Petting of a fit, active tortoise will normally produce a sudden pulling in of its legs and head, accompanied by an aggressive hiss.

Careful observation and tests, particularly with blind tortoises, reveal that a tortoise can sort out food plants from non-food plants solely by smell. They also can follow a scent trail as well as any bloodhound. Pregnant females sniff potential nest sites and subsequently choose only those where the soil temperature is within acceptable limits. The obvious inference is that the soil temperature is checked by smell.

This acute sense enables the tortoise to do some things that are impossible to humans. In still air a tortoise can "see" humans, tortoises, and other animals on the far side of an opaque screen and even can recognise them as individuals—a very useful thing to be able to do if you are hiding from a predator and want to know if it is safe to come out. If it is necessary to raise a head to see if the predator has gone, it may turn out to be the last opportunity the animal has to raise its head! Scent trails left by other tortoises can be followed, which helps in the rapid finding of the best basking, feeding, or hiding places and aids finding possible mates or competitors.

Touch

Some owners seem to think that because tortoises have hard shells and are covered with scales they have no sense of touch. This plainly is untrue. If given an injection, the tortoise will wince just like a human. If they had no sense of touch through their carapaces they would hardly knock against each other in their territorial and amatory activities. Any careful observer can watch responses to a variety of tactile inputs. The fact that tortoises are incapable of making a noise when in pain has had unfortunate consequences in the past, when unthinking people concluded wrongly that no sound meant no pain. However, times appear to be improving. For example, one sees few tethered tortoises these days.

If you wish to understand your tortoise's senses and behaviour better, watch it carefully, but at the same time be still, quiet, and patient so that the tortoise forgets you are watching. You cannot expect any animal to behave naturally when something 40 times its size is hovering nearby! Do not expect the tortoise to understand your motives, since you probably do not understand his!

Giant tortoises on the reserve in Santa Cruz, Galapagos.

BEHAVIOUR

Some animals, such as antelopes, are herd animals, and their instincts lead them to congregate in large groups for safety. Some animals, such as hyenas, are pack animals; their instincts lead them to cooperate in small groups for combined hunting. Some animals, such as macaws, form strong pair bonds. As human beings, we share all these instincts in varying degrees. We can understand, more or less, the kinds of forces that drive these instincts, if not always their intensity.

The instincts of Mediterranean tortoises are different from all these. They are solitary, territorial animals. A tortoise's overriding instincts are to control a territory and to persuade other tortoises to leave. Humans seem to have great difficulty in understanding these instincts even when the evidence is very powerful. Most tortoise owners try to attach human emotions and feelings to tortoises, but comparatively simple behavioural experiments will show the error of this. For example, I frequently am told "My tortoise is eating less because he is pining for a mate," or some similar statement. However, in *every* comparative trial that I have done or have seen done using comparable healthy or comparable sick animals, solitary animals *always* eat more than animals in groups! In the following pages I will attempt to present a comprehensive picture of *Testudo graeca* behaviour that fits with observations made over the past 12 years.

EXPLORATION BEHAVIOUR

Assuming that it is warm and healthy, a solitary tortoise in a new area will explore the area fully, looking for (or, more accurately, smelling for) food plants, hiding places, and, most importantly, the best basking spots. This exploration phase takes about a year. In following years the tortoise uses its memory and hence becomes much more efficient at being in the right place at the right time. This process has two main consequences. First, if a tortoise is moved it suffers a setback. It is therefore much better if one

intends to go on holiday during the summer to find someone to look after your pets in their normal home rather than to transport them to a new home for a fortnight. Second, when a tortoise has learned all the right places to go for all its needs, it becomes very attached to the territory. If a newcomer is introduced the owner of the territory will make the newcomer feel as unwelcome as possible.

TERRITORIAL BEHAVIOUR

This normally consists of chasing, "butting," and biting. These instincts are much stronger in males than females, and are much stronger between "strangers" than between long standing companions. Occasionally tortoises will use other tactics. A small but aggressive tortoise that realises it cannot win a "butting" match with a larger opponent sometimes will attempt to overturn the opponent or will try to harry it from a blind spot.

For an adult male tortoise, territorial ownership is essential. He needs somewhere to bask, somewhere to hide, and growing plants to eat. He defends his territory energetically, butting the rear of an intruder's carapace with the front of his plastron. If this proves insufficient, he will bite any exposed limbs or sometimes the head or neck. If the intruder responds by running, he is chased off. If he responds by withdrawing his head and legs, he is forced to suffer the final humiliation of being mounted. This way the tortoise maintains his grip on his territory, which he also paints with scent trails to advertise the fact that it is indeed his. As he grows he needs more food and hence a bigger area, and provided he can control a large enough food supply he will continue to grow.

Females also sometimes behave in exactly the same way even to mounting and "mating." This has led to considerable confusion among some owners who, assuming that the behaviour was sexual, have decided either that females were males or that they owned "gay" tortoises!

HIERARCHIAL BEHAVIOUR

In undisturbed wild colonies of Mediterranean tortoises, the maximum observed population density is about 80 tortoises per hectare (i.e., about 150 sq. yards per tortoise—including hatchlings). In captivity, tortoises are normally kept at higher population densities, sometimes enormously so. This has a significant effect on behaviour.

In a confined area, such as a suburban garden, long-term territorial behaviour is impossible and the loser in territorial disputes has nowhere to go. This is normally, but by no means exclusively, solved by hierarchy. Stronger and fitter animals become dominant. They reinforce this dominance by butting, mounting, and ejaculating on less dominant animals, who respond by giving the dominant animals a wide berth and allowing them first choice of basking areas, food, and females.

One interesting observation is that if soil is dug within the tortoises' range the non-dominant tortoises will not normally go near it until the dominant (usually male) animal explores it and covers it with his scent trails.

SEXUAL BEHAVIOUR

In the wild, when boy meets girl the initial reaction is "get off my territory." However, sexually mature females give off a smell that creates a sexual response from the male. His actions change, and he attempts to immobilise and then mount the female. If he is successful, penetration and ejaculation take place. While ejaculating the male opens his mouth wide and makes a high pitched "mewing" noise. After this has happened the female normally escapes. The sexual smell appears to be operative only over a short range, and once the female is separated and out of sight it is all over. This behaviour occurs at infrequent, irregular intervals throughout the year, but frequency is higher in spring and autumn. This behaviour is very similar to the territorial and hierarchical behaviour previously described, to the extent that many human observers attribute all these behaviour patterns to sex. Careful observation, however, reveals subtle differences. When pursuing females the male will try to prevent escape rather than encourage it. Males will bite a female's back legs to prevent her escape for sexual reasons, but in territorial battles the bites are for real and can be directed at any part of the victim's anatomy. In particular, bites directed at the head always appear to be a sign of territorial conflict.

There are differences between the behaviours of males, females, pregnant females, and hatchlings and between healthy and sick tortoises.

A) Males

Healthy male tortoises often are incredibly aggressive. It is necessary to have separate accommodations for each male, or at least accommodations available so that males can be split up if necessary.

B) Females and Hatchlings

Compared to the males, females and hatchlings are placid and can be kept in groups. They will accept shared facilities, each going about their own business and totally ignoring the others. Fighting normally is a problem only if a stranger is introduced, and even then it normally becomes unacceptable only if the newcomer is sick and the sitting tenant(s) is dominant.

In the wild, immediately after hatching, baby tortoises go about the business of finding food and calcium, basking, and hibernating. A change of behavior pattern occurs, particularly for males, at the onset of sexual maturity, which normally happens at about five years of age. Territorial instincts appear to surface first, and later sexual instincts.

BEHAVIOR IN CAPTIVITY

Obviously all of the behaviour I have discussed also happens in captivity. However, there are differences due to proximity and state of health. In general, in captivity tortoises are kept in much closer contact with each other than would be the case in the wild, and this modifies their behaviour. Healthy males frequently will fight obsessively because the loser can no longer escape the victor. Sometimes this will go on indefinitely, and a hierarchy is formed whereby the winner gets the best basking spots, first choice of available food, and access to all the females. The loser in return doesn't get beaten up. It's a hard life!

In the wild, once mating has occurred and the couple have parted, the female goes her own way. However, in the confined areas of captivity the female scent is everywhere and males with the scent always in their nostrils will continuously attempt intercourse and not eat or allow the female(s) to eat.

These aberrations of natural behaviour obviously detract from the well-being of the group. Non-dominant males suffer because they are deprived of basking facilities and food. Dominant males suffer because they do not eat enough. Females suffer because they are not allowed time to bask or eat. Unless special housing is provided to reduce this aberrant behaviour, the general condition of the group will decline.

Behavioural interactions decrease as the physical condition of the tortoises decreases. They then will live "happily" together but with reduced activity and will demonstrate few of the behaviour patterns I have been describing. This situation of sub-optimal but relatively stable health and minimal behaviour patterns is very common in mixed captive groups that I have seen. It is important to

realise that if a tortoise in poor health is introduced into an existing community these behaviour patterns will put the newcomer at a considerable disadvantage.

Behaviour, in particular sexual behaviour, becomes more complicated if different species are kept together. Male *Testudo graeca*, for instance, will attempt to mate with female *Testudo hermanni*, but this appears to cause the female *hermanni* considerable distress.

RECOMMENDATIONS

Many owners indicate that they do this or that to ensure that their tortoises are "happy." The only objective way that I know of telling if a tortoise is "happy" is if its behaviour is normal, i.e., the behaviour is the same as it would be in the wild, unmodified by captivity. This is hard to achieve, but I feel it is worth striving for. The following items will help. Keep only one species, and preferably only one subspecies, of tortoise. Keep males and females separately, putting them together for short periods if you want them to mate. Separate areas can be provided for behavioural, hygiene, or medical reasons. If you keep a variety of species, it becomes increasingly difficult both to keep the tortoises in good health and to obtain anything resembling natural behaviour.

Most human observers tend to ascribe every interaction between tortoises to sex. I hope that you will see after reading this chapter that this says more about the observers than the tortoises!

Courtship displayed by two *Testudo graeca*.

BREEDING

Tortoise sex is very different from mammalian sex and it is important to understand the differences even if you do not wish to breed because fatal problems can occur if one does not do the right things.

For some mammals, for example sheep, it is important that all offspring should be born in spring, partly because when offspring are born together they suffer fewer losses from predators, and partly because they then have a full season's feeding before facing the rigours of winter. Sheep achieve this partly by having a sexual cycle tied to the annual seasons and partly by being herd animals, so all mating is carried out at the appropriate time.

Tortoises have a similar problem but for different reasons, and they have solved it in a different way. They need to lay their eggs in spring or early summer because they need the warmth of the summer sun to hatch them, but they cannot use the mammalian system because they are solitary, not herd animals, so they cannot synchronise their intercourse. They have solved this problem by having a variable length of pregnancy and laying their eggs according to the season and climate.

Tortoises meet and mate in the wild at infrequent, irregular intervals throughout the year. The mating results in a batch of 20 or 30 eggs being impregnated. These eggs are passed down the tubes of the female in clutches of two to ten eggs. The eggs grow to full size and then the shells are secreted over them. This means that an X-ray can be taken before the shells are on and the plate will show no visible sign of any eggs, then two weeks later an X-ray can show a large clutch of fully formed eggs.

It is difficult to be sure about gestation periods, but I believe the shortest length of gestation (period from fertilisation to laying of the eggs) to be about 55 days and the longest period resulting in fertile eggs to be about 30 months. There is no limit to the length of time that eggs can be carried. I have proof of five years and believable reports of 20 years. Eggs kept inside the female for these lengths of time are understandably infertile as they become over-calcified. Each year another layer of calcium is added so that the shells become thicker and their surfaces become rougher. This process is inevitable if male and female tortoises are kept together and if facilities are not provided to enable the female to lay her eggs. I am always amazed to hear owners who keep males and females together say "I don't want to breed my tortoises"—as though somehow the owner's desires would change the tortoises's biology!

PREGNANT BEHAVIOUR

When a female has complete eggs inside her, her behaviour changes.

1) Even when obviously healthy and alert she eats significantly less food, presumably because the eggs take up abdominal space so she no longer feels hungry.

2) If kept with other tortoises, she becomes aggressive and attempts to establish, temporarily, a dominant position. She normally will pick the largest tortoise around and start butting and mounting. She does this because she needs to be left undisturbed to lay her eggs, and if she is aggressive enough the other tortoises will give her a wide berth. Immediately after laying she becomes passive again. One consequence of this behaviour is that a female normally will not lay if there is a dominant male in her territory because he will not allow her to become dominant. Another consequence is that even if one has an area that is totally adequate in every way for egg laying, it is pointless to put a strange pregnant female in it hoping that she will lay. In general she will not. She will feel vulnerable among the resident population, and even if they are removed she will still be aware of all their scent trails and will still not feel safe enough to lay. Generally it takes 12 months in a suitable area for a tortoise to feel sufficiently at home to become dominant and consequently lay her eggs.

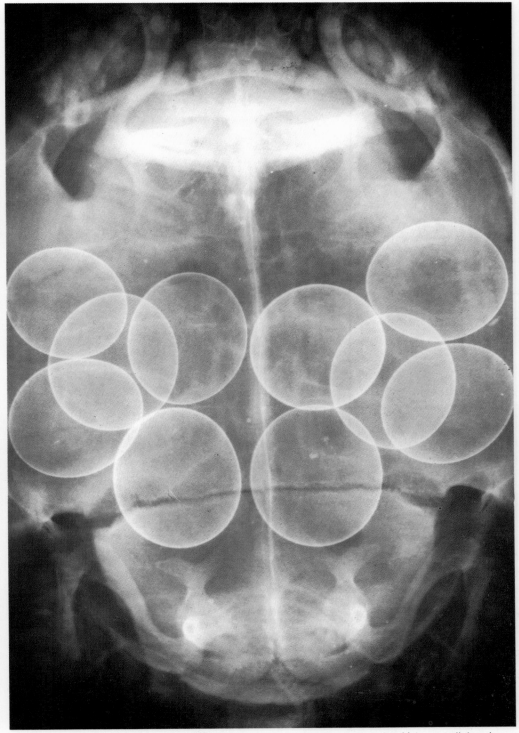

X-rays of eggs can be misleading since the tortoise eggs are transparent to X-rays until they have shells. This female has 10 eggs which are shelled; she might have as many as 20 more eggs which have not become shelled. Photo by the author.

3) She enormously increases exploratory behaviour. Many owners lose tortoises because of escapes when this happens.

4) She sometimes exhibits reflex digging actions with her back legs. This only happens when the tortoise is very warm and then only occasionally.

The female will lay only if a series of conditions is correct. If *any* condition is wrong she will retain her eggs until *all* conditions are correct. In the wild this means she has to find the *right* site in late spring or early summer.

Eggs forming later in the year are retained in her body over hibernation and then laid in the spring. In captivity in northern Europe, this means she will lay only in exceptional circumstances unless the appropriate conditions are manufactured for her. The required conditions are:

1) minimum one year knowledge of territory;

2) ability to attain dominance;

3) right time of the year;

4) diggable soil;

5) soil not too cold;

6) soil not too hot;

7) soil not too wet;

8) soil not too dry.

The way the tortoise deals with items 1 and 2 has already been explained. A tortoise's laying mechanisms appear to be triggered by the production of a hormone called oxytocin. I assume, but cannot prove, that production of this substance is blocked when daylight hours begin to shorten.

If items 1, 2, and 3 are acceptable, the tortoise searches for a suitable nest site. She looks for an area with bare earth (item 4) that is raised above the general ground level and is therefore well-drained so the humidity in the nest will not become excessive (item 7).

She then smells the soil. If there is a crust on the soil, some tortoises will scrape away the surface with their front claws and smell again. If the soil's surface temperature is too hot or too cold the tortoise will continue its search for a suitable site. If the temperature is approximately 30°C (86°F) (items 5 and 6), she attempts to dig a nest.

She uses her front claws as anchors and digs with her back claws. Tortoises normally dig with their front claws, but in these circumstances they dig with their back claws. She digs with an outward circular motion of the hind legs and attempts to dig an undercut nest. This is possible only if the soil is slightly moist. If the soil is too dry the sides of the nest will collapse, or it will be too hard to dig at all. In either case she will abandon the attempt and look elsewhere (item 4). This process has previously been described as digging a "trial nest." I do not believe this explanation. If the soil conditions are right the first time, the tortoise will lay the first time.

When the nest has been dug to the tortoise's satisfaction, her eggs are laid one at a time. Each egg is laid in the rear of the nest, then she pushes that one to the front of the nest with her hind legs. This ensures that the nest space is clear for the next egg to be laid, thus reducing the risk of breakage. Also, because the eggs are wet with the female's body fluids, this action coats each egg with a thin layer of soil. This has the effect of slightly separating the eggs from each other within the nest, which means that if one egg subsequently goes bad it does not affect the other eggs.

The tortoise then reverses her digging action, moving her hind legs in wide inward circular movements to cover the eggs and fill the nest. At the same time she very slowly swings her body from side to side, pivoting on her anchored front legs so that she can reach every scrap of excavated soil, her plastron smoothing over the refilled nest. This results in the nest being almost undetectable after she has finished. The whole process of digging, laying, and covering normally takes two to four hours. Immediately afterward the tortoise appears exhausted, but she soon recovers to become ravenously hungry.

Once a clutch of eggs is laid, another clutch is separated from the store of impregnated eggs and the process is started again. The process of egg laying is totally under the influence of climatic conditions, and although mating is necessary from time to time to top up the store of impregnated eggs, once the store exists the female can go on laying fertile eggs for years without further mating. In the wild, *Testudo graeca* females are always pregnant and lay two or three batches of eggs each season.

When the climate is right this system works beautifully. However, when kept in a northern European climate, problems are inevitable. In the wild, conditions for egg laying are acceptable for three or four months in the year. In England, south of a line joining London and Bristol, conditions are normally acceptable for about one week in the year. Further north the conditions are never correct. These generalisations can be modified by mini-climatic conditions in an individual place and obviously will change with weather conditions for any particular year. However, for most of northern Europe, most of the time, females will not lay but retain their eggs within their bodies.

Eggs retained by a female for up to two years generally present no problem. However, retained eggs are given an extra coating of calcium each year. This results in the egg shells becoming steadily thicker and rougher. This roughness means that if climatic conditions become correct and the tortoise tries to lay, the results can be tragic. The fallopian tube walls can be split and/or the egg can pass into the bladder. In other circumstances the egg(s) can become diseased and the disease spread to the tortoise (egg peritonitis). When any of these conditions occur, the female changes from apparently perfect health to death very rapidly, sometimes within 48 hours.

It is *very* important, if one does not provide suitable conditions to enable females to lay their eggs, that males and females be kept separately and that an X-ray examination of the females is carried out every three or four years to check that they are free of eggs.

EGG FERTILITY

It has been common practice to keep different species and subspecies of tortoise in one group. While this has obvious advantages in saving human labour, it can lead to both behavioural and breeding problems. The major breeding problem is cross-fertilization between species and subspecies. In general, if unmatched species mate together, infertile eggs are produced and the likelihood of pregnancy problems is increased. If the female is subsequently mated with a matching male she will continue to produce clutches of infertile eggs until all the eggs from the first mating are used up, then the eggs will become fertile. This can take several years. Interestingly, this problem is most acute when groups of 2 to 12 tortoises are kept together, and appears to be less of a problem when 30 or more are involved, presumably because it is easier for a male to find an acceptable mate.

Some authorities have quoted a small fertility rate for mating between differing species and 10% fertility for mating between differing subspecies. In contrast, my experience in this field leads me to believe that the fertility rate between differing species is virtually nil and the fertility rate between different subspecies is on the order of 1%. It is very easy to be misled when studying fertility because, unless one takes extreme precautions, one cannot be sure who is the father of a particular batch of eggs. As should be clear after reading this chapter, it is *not* sufficient only to know the mating history of the mother over the last year or so. Once a pair have been successfully identified and have proved to be compatible, the fertility rate can be very high (95% or more).

Fertility reduces if: 1) the pair's state of health is reduced; 2) the diet is inadequate (in particular pregnant females need quite high levels of calcium intake); 3) the pair are inadequately hibernated (in particular the male's sperm count is reduced unless adequately hibernated).

RECOMMENDED BREEDING PROCEDURE

Make sure all tortoises are kept in as good a state of health as possible.

Keep males and females in two separate enclosures, each with all the necessary facilities.

Keep females away from all males for

Tortoises are most easily sexed by details of the tail length and position of the vent. This female *Testado hermanni* has a short tail and a downward-facing vent. Note the large scale at the end of the tail and the absence of thigh spurs, both characteristics of *T. hermanni*. Photos by Isabelle Francais, with the assistance of Mr. Abbott.

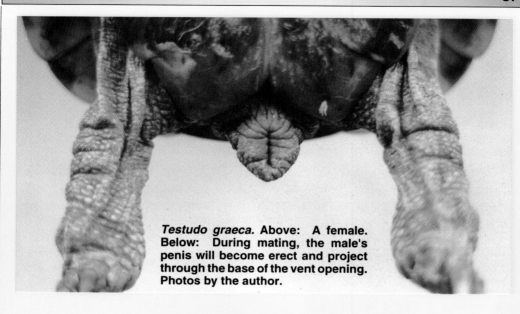

Testudo graeca. Above: A female. Below: During mating, the male's penis will become erect and project through the base of the vent opening. Photos by the author.

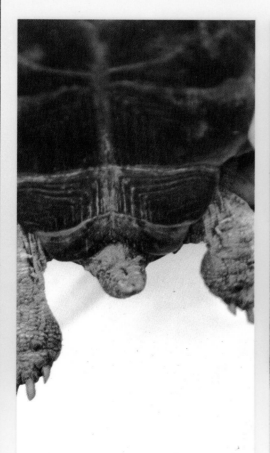

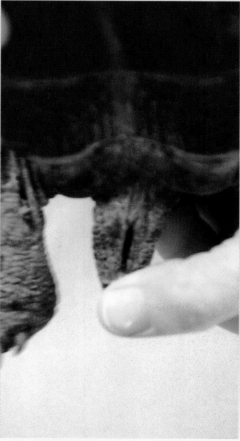

at least a year, then get them X-rayed to ensure that they are free of eggs from any previous mating. If eggs are present, have laying induced, wait another year, X-ray again, and if necessary, induce again. Repeat until the female is clear.

In a separate mating enclosure, put a male of matched species, subspecies, and race together with a female that has been cleared of possible eggs from unmatched matings. Two hours a day for four or five days is normally about right, but it depends on the individuals.

Make sure the female has access to a larger than normal amount of calcium.

Watch the female carefully for the symptoms of pregnancy described earlier. If you suspect pregnancy, try to get her to lay. In general, unless females are definitely not pregnant, they should lay every year, either naturally or by artificial induction.

ARTIFICIAL INDUCTION METHOD

Go to a vet, keeping the tortoise as warm as possible before and during the journey. Ask the vet to:

1) X-ray the tortoise;
2) count the eggs;
3) put the tortoise in a box with a basking lamp (preferably a reflector bulb);
4) inject with oxytocin;
5) remain in attendance while the eggs are laid and remove each egg as it is laid;
6) put the eggs in a box surrounded by cotton, wool, or some similar material.

If the tortoise is left unattended when laying by this method, reflex digging and egg moving actions by her back legs are likely to break the eggs. Artificial induction as described above will not affect the fertility or otherwise of the eggs. If the eggs are overcalcified this method, rather than natural laying, is often essential to remove the eggs. If the above process is not successful, or only partially successful, it is normally best to wait a few weeks and then try again.

In extreme cases it is possible to use other veterinary techniques. It sometimes happens, particularly if crossbreeding has taken place, that eggs can be formed which are too large to pass through the pelvic girdle. This can be diagnosed by careful measurement of X-rays. It is possible, if the eggs can be persuaded by inductions to take up the right positions, for the eggs to be surgically broken via the cloaca, thus facilitating their removal.

Although any competent vet should be able to carry out these techniques, it is generally preferable to go to a reptile specialist. They will be much more familiar with the problems involved and will have the appropriate equipment on their premises.

NATURAL LAYING METHOD

One needs to get *all*, yes *all*, not most, of the conditions listed earlier in this chapter correct in order to get the females to lay. It is quite a lot of effort, but the thrill of success makes it seem no trouble at all!!

A few tips:

1) Keep females in small groups in familiar territory with access to a laying area—they need to feel "at home."
2) Keep males out. Females can't become dominant when a male wants his "wicked way."
3) Don't leave soil and other temperatures to chance—measure them.
4) In south-facing, sheltered gardens in southern England it normally is possible to achieve 30°C (86°F) soil temperatures naturally for a short period in the year. Elsewhere some form of soil heating is essential.
5) The tortoise needs to be *constantly warm*. She normally will lay only if 35°C (95°F) basking facilities are available *plus* an air temperature of 25°C (77°F) *plus* lamps over the laying area to give a surface temperature of 30°C (86°F). If one can get a tortoise into the habit of laying, she will lay when the conditions are not correct, but ideal conditions are needed to get her started. It is preferable to ensure by means of lamps, timers, heaters, and thermostats that ideal conditions exist for two months in early summer.

If one understands the necessary requirements, it is possible to devise several different ways of achieving natural laying.

For example, one can heat up a box (about a 12-inch [30 cm] cube) of peat to about 30°C (86°F) using a reflector lamp, checking with a suitable thermometer. At the same time, one gets the pregnant tortoise sufficiently warm that she starts reflex digging motions with her back legs. Put the tortoise on the box and she should then dig and lay. This method is quick and easy but does require considerable observation skills in order to get the timing right.

I live sufficiently far north (in the west midlands) that tortoises will not lay naturally in the garden in spite of many schemes I have tried. Therefore, in order to try to produce as natural a setup as possible, I have converted a greenhouse into a laying area. The greenhouse is within the run that is available to the pregnant female tortoises, and in general they have free access to it at all times. Occasionally the door is closed to prevent other tortoises from disturbing one that is attempting to lay, but this normally is not essential because the tortoises's own instincts cope with this.

If one uses a greenhouse, it is important to provide sun screens and artificial heating because directly using the sun for warmth produces widely fluctuating temperatures, and steady temperatures are essential for consistent success. It also is necessary to water the area regularly or the soil will become too dry to be acceptable to the tortoises.

After laying, the eggs are carefully dug up and incubated.

Testudo hermanni demonstrating its climbing ability. Photo by the author.

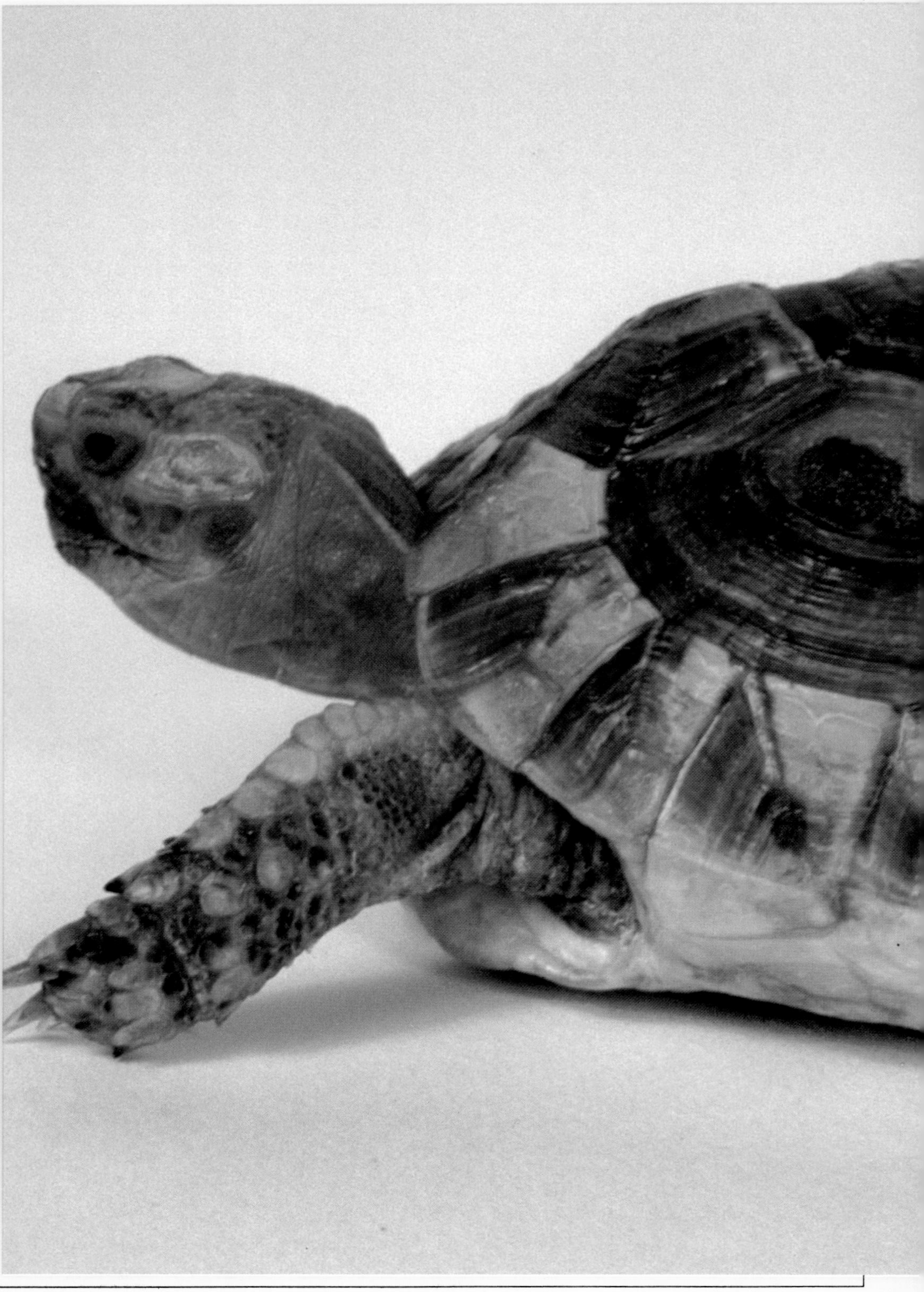

Testudo graeca, a portrait by Isabelle Francais.

INCUBATION

When I first attempted to incubate eggs I had remarkably little success, and at the same time I would have people telling me "I have just hatched three eggs. I put them in the airing cupboard and they hatched." Very frustrating! However, no one seemed to know why sometimes they succeeded and sometimes they failed or why their setup worked and mine failed. Also, no one appeared to have taken anywhere near enough measurements so that their setups could be copied with any semblance of accuracy.

In order to find out what conditions were necessary, I carried out a series of tests and tried several different ways to achieve these conditions. I came to the conclusion that the following conditions were necessary:

1) Eggs must come from the mating of compatible subspecies. This does NOT refer to the last mating or to a mating that happened so many weeks before; it refers to the mating that produced the impregnated eggs.

2) The eggs must be recent, i.e., not overcalcified.

3) The female must get a reasonably large amount of calcium in her diet while the eggs are forming. If not, the growing embryo can suffer from osteodystrophy (soft bones and carapace) and hence be unable to break out of the egg shell.

4) The temperature during incubation should be between 26°C (79°F) and 34°C (93°F).

5) The humidity during incubation should not exceed 95% for more than 15 minutes. If this happens, water passes through the egg shell and can drown the embryo. This is not critical in the early stages of incubation.

6) The humidity during incubation should not be less than 50%. Low humidity leads to loss of water from the egg. If a small amount is lost, the hatchling will be smaller than normal. If a large amount of water is lost the egg contents solidify and an embryo does not form.

7) The eggs should be kept with the same surface up after the embryo begins to form. For the first week or so the eggs

can be juggled with no ill effects, the exact length of time being dependent on temperature. The embryo forms on top of the yolk and subsequent turning of the egg leaves the embryo upside down and smothered by its yolk sac. This is often, but not invariably, fatal.

In the wild, the temperature and humidity conditions are achieved partly by the skill of the tortoise in choosing a nest site and partly by the scale of the natural environment. A limestone hillside gains or loses both temperature and humidity at a very slow rate, so that if a tortoise chooses an appropriate nest site, the conditions at that site will remain substantially constant over the time it takes to hatch the eggs. This, unfortunately, is not necessarily the case when one tries to achieve incubation artificially.

Most previous publications recommend an incubation setup that appears to mimic natural conditions. That is, burying the eggs in soil or some other medium, using a heater and thermostat to get the temperature correct, and using either an adjacent bowl of water or spraying to achieve the correct humidity. If a setup like this works for you, fine; carry on. However, my experience using this kind of apparatus is that the temperature control works beautifully, but the humidity control requires more skill than I am consistently capable of supplying. This results in a poor hatching rate and a lot of problems.

Finally, I modified a bird egg incubator, and suddenly it was easy. The eggs are kept on a grid suspended in air. This means that the temperature control is harder and problems caused by power cuts or accidental disconnection are made more acute. However, this is more than offset by the fact that humidity is much easier to control and measure. Bird eggs normally incubate at about 37°C (98°F); tortoise eggs normally incubate at about 30°C (86°F). When the temperature is reduced, less water is evaporated from the humidity trays. To obtain the correct humidity levels, I found that increasing the surface area of the water by a factor of about three did the trick. As with all other aspects of tortoise care, measurement is vital for consistent results. Check the temperature and humidity often.

INCUBATION METHOD

1) Set up and switch on the incubator. Adjust and leave running for long enough to ensure that the temperature and humidity are correct and steady.

2) Dig up eggs from the laying area very carefully and as soon after laying as possible.

3) *Carefully* clean the eggs using a warm damp cloth.

4) *Carefully* dry the eggs with a dry cloth.

5) Weigh the eggs (to an accuracy of 0.1 gm).

6) Using a soft pencil, mark the egg with code letters or numbers so each egg can recognised.

7) Put the eggs in the incubator with the markings uppermost.

8) Record all information.

Checks can be made on the progress of the incubation by two methods: weighing and candling. In my trials I made extensive use of both methods with no apparent ill effects. However, any checking is obviously potentially damaging and should be done infrequently and with great care.

EGG WEIGHT CHECKING

Egg shells are semi-permeable. In normal incubation conditions eggs slowly lose water to their surroundings. Overcalcified eggs lose water very slowly indeed. With normal calcification, infertile eggs lose water faster than fertile eggs. Hence, if regular weighings are taken of a batch of eggs and graphs of weight against time are plotted, it is possible to separate infertile from fertile eggs. The actual weight loss depends on the temperature and humidity in the incubator. Eggs normally will fail to hatch if they lose 25% or more of their weight during incubation.

EGG CANDLING

If a light from a small bright source is shone on an egg and the egg is observed from the other side, objects inside can be seen. Translucent objects are illuminated and opaque objects can be seen as shadows. A pinpoint light source can be made by using a post card with a quarter-inch hole cut in it held in front of a light bulb. Observations can be made horizontally or vertically. The theory is easy, practice and interpretation difficult.

First, eggs should be kept the right way up at all times. Second, light bulbs are hot and one must avoid temperature changes, therefore the time for observation, particularly in the vertical position, must be minimised.

INTERPRETATION

One is observing mostly semi-liquid contents using light that has passed through fairly solid egg shells. Varying egg shell thicknesses and textures add to the confusion of what one can see. However, in general terms, infertile eggs either remain liquid throughout, liquid with an air space above, or the contents solidify to form a semi-opaque mass in the lower part of the egg. Fertile eggs initially form blood vessels in the area that becomes the yolk sac and then an embryo tortoise grows transversely at the top of the egg. Viewed from above, the legs, head, and tail can be clearly seen in shadow.

This can be summed up as follows:

opaque mass at the top of the egg means fertile;

opaque mass at the bottom of the egg means infertile;

shadowy shapes and lines mean—your guess is as good as anyone else's!

HATCHLING SEX DETERMINATION

Sex determination in tortoises uses a totally different method from the human one, with which most of us have become familiar. In humans the sex of an offspring is determined at conception by a random joining of parental chromosomes.

Pioneering experiments by Claude Pieau in France showed that the eggs of *Testudo graeca* are sexless when laid, and that the sex of the offspring is determined by the temperature at which the eggs are incubated. This is called "environmental sex determination."

1

1. *Alpha*, three weeks old, in the author's hand.

2. *Rosie* laying her eggs in the hole she dug in the earth.

3. *Alpha* at his third birthday party looks healthy and alert. The second and third annual rings are clear though the first is difficult to see. Note the rounded carapace and almost total lack of pyramiding of the scutes.

4. *Rosie*, having laid six eggs, now moves the eggs around to tidy them before she covers them with the earth. All photos by the author.

2

4

3

Eggs from a single female may number up to 30, laid in two or three batches of six to eight eggs each year. The eggs are in an incubator which ensures the proper temperature and humidity.

Over-calcification of the egg shell is a common abnormality among captive tortoises. Tortoise eggs are smooth like a chicken egg, and not leathery.

Tortoises mating.

A new hatchling of *Testudo graeca*, only a few hours old. With it is a normal egg and a match box to show relative size of both the egg and the hatchling.
All photos by the author.

In more detail, Dr. Pieau's experiments indicate that sex in tortoises appears to be determined by the temperature of the growing embryo when the gonads are being formed about 15 to 30 days after laying. It is possible that gonads that start developing as male can change to female if the incubation temperature rises, but the reverse cannot happen. My observations totally confirm the principal but do not totally confirm the detail. In particular, inexperienced owners who tend to incubate at fluctuating temperatures tend to hatch males. I find it requires consistently accurate temperature settings to produce females. However, since it takes five years to sex living juvenile tortoises with any degree of confidence, and my apparatus was not initially accurate enough to quote temperatures with accuracy over the full period of incubation, experimental error could well explain the differences in observations.

In general terms, at temperatures around 30°C (86°F) sex tends to be random; above that temperature females form; below that temperature males form. Above 35°C (95°F) deformed hatchings are more likely and death inside the egg shell more frequent. About 25°C (77°F) is the lowest temperature at which eggs will hatch. Incubation time varies with temperature, being about 55 days at 35°C (95°F), 70 days at 30°C (86°F), and 120 days at 25°C (77°F). I suggest you use a steady 33°C (92°F) if you wish to hatch females and 27°C (81°F) if you wish to hatch males.

If you are in doubt as to which to hatch, may I suggest you try for females? This is for several reasons. First, females in northern Europe have a higher comparative death rate because of pregnancy problems. Second, females are more amenable to being kept in groups. Third, for future breeding it is perfectly possible for one male to service very large numbers of females.

HATCHING

As a fertile egg develops, the yolk sac steadily shrinks in size and the embryo steadily grows. The embryo grows transversely across the top of the egg. At full term the plastron is folded across its centre and the carapace is pressed firmly against the inside of the shell, to the extent that the "orange peel" texture of the inside of the shell is imprinted on the carapace. At this time the yolk sac runs out of nourishment and the hatchling begins to open and close its mouth, an action presumably caused by reflex hunger reaction. Because the hatchling has an "egg tooth" on the tip of its nose and its nose is pressed against the egg shell, this action results in the cutting of a small slot in the egg shell. This slot considerably weakens the shell and also allows the egg contents to dry out. The body of the hatchling then straightens out—like a flower opening. The weakened shell then breaks and the new hatchling climbs out.

To correct several current misconceptions:

1) Embryos never grow axially in the egg. If they did, they would find it almost impossible to break out.

2) Twins do occur, but very rarely.

3) Tortoises do not break out of their eggshells by pushing with their hind legs, clawing with their front legs, or biting a hole. The motive power is not muscular but carapace straightening.

4) Eggs from one clutch do not necessarily hatch simultaneously.

Owners of wild tortoises have stated that all members of a clutch do hatch together. This is definitely not the case with incubated eggs that I have observed. The differences in these observations may be due to poor observation in the wild or poor temperature control in my experiments. Whatever the explanation, advice has been offered that if an egg does not hatch within a few days of others in the same batch it should be opened to free the trapped tortoise. I broke an egg under these circumstances to find a three-quarters grown hatchling with yolk sac still attached. I kept the tortoise plus the yolk sac in hygienic conditions at 30°C (86°F) only to see the umbilical cord shrivel and the tortoise steadily lose condition. I decided she was becoming dehydrated and succeeded in persuading

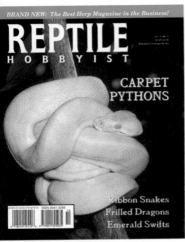

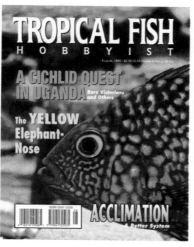

her to take some water plus glucose from a teaspoon while keeping her in a hen's egg shell. Eventually I succeeded in persuading her to eat. I cut the umbilical cord and she slowly got a grip on life. However, her carapace was slightly deformed and her development was put back several months. I repeated the experiment with another tortoise 12 months later with identical results.

Feeding a semi-comatose 6 gm (0.2 oz) dehydrated baby tortoise is not exactly easy. I would therefore recommend that eggs be left to incubate to full term. If one is sure the embryo is full-grown and the yolk sac fully absorbed, it probably is reasonable to break the egg, but it should not be necessary and carries added risks. Hatchlings from artificially broken eggs are invariably smaller than their naturally hatched siblings. A theory has been suggested to me that a growth hormone is the last thing to be absorbed from the yolk sac before hatching. This would explain the observed facts.

HATCHLING CARE

There are no differences whatsoever in the conditions or diet required by hatchlings compared with adults. The only problems arise from the fact that if anything is wrong the effects are much quicker to show themselves.

The easiest way to keep hatchlings is in an open-topped box with a 40 watt 30° angle reflector bulb to provide a warm spot of 35°C (95°F) in part of their box during daylight hours. Keeping the box in a centrally heated house will provide the necessary background air temperature of about 20 to 25°C (68 to 77°F) during the day and 15 to 20°C (59 to 68°F) during the night.

Diet is critical, especially calcium. Calcium must be fed from the first meal. If the diet you are feeding is not right, the condition of adults declines impercepti-

bly. The same wrong diet fed to hatchlings generally causes rapid decline. The most common mistake is to feed a diet too rich in protein and too short in calcium. The calcium/protein ratio is important. If it is just too low, the hatchlings grow too quickly and the scutes become deformed into pyramidal shapes, but the tortoise will survive.

If the ratio is slightly worse, the pyramidal deformations are worse, and the bone forming these shapes becomes hollow, taking up space that otherwise would be occupied by the lungs. This means the condition of the tortoise steadily declines and death frequently occurs, generally from bronchial disorders at about 18 to 24 months old.

If the ratio is worse still, the edges of the hatchling's mouth do not harden. The tortoise then cannot bite the more fibrous foods and is forced to choose softer, more protein-rich food, further lowering the calcium/protein ratio. This is obviously a one-way road. Hatchlings caught in this downward spiral normally die of malnutrition in one to three months.

Hatchlings weakened by incorrect diet generally have inadequate immune systems and are prone to disease problems, such as runny noses. At the time of writing, incorrect diet is, by a very large percentage, the largest primary cause of hatchling death.

I have found that hatchlings with soft mouths can be cured in about three weeks by opening their mouths with a cocktail stick and, using an artist's brush, feeding them with neat powdered cuttlebone or limestone flour. This, together with a calcium-rich diet, often works miracles. Initially, one often needs to use a soft food with small leaves that they can handle (cress is ideal) and steadily change to better, high-fibre foods (such as dandelion) as their mouths harden.

A portrait of *Testudo hermanni*. Photo by Isabelle Francais.

Tortoises are best kept alone except for mating purposes.

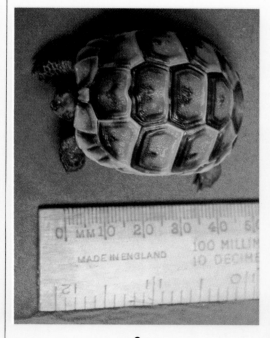

3

2

4

1

1. A six-month-old *Testudo graeca* hatchling about 2 inches long.

2. The same six-month-old hatchling about 40 mm wide (25.4 mm = 1 inch).

3. The same six-month-old hatchling has an almost circular carapace. Note the growth around each scute.

4. The normal coloration of the author's pet *Alpha*. The plastron coloration is very variable.

Photos by the author.

GROWTH & AGE

Humans grow until they reach sexual maturity, then the body chemistry dramatically changes. Hormones are produced that stop growth. Tortoises do not have this mechanism. Provided:

1) the tortoise is kept in an adequate thermal environment so that it can keep its body temperature correct;

2) it has adequate quality and quantity of food, vitamins, and calcium;

3) it does not spend too large a percentage of its time in sexual or territorial activity; and

4) it is healthy;

it will continue to live and grow indefinitely. Many people are very skeptical about this statement because it differs so markedly from human experience, but it is the only explanation I can offer that fits the observations.

Carapace growth occurs at the margins of each scute, but mainly at the lower margins of the costal scutes. When kept in ideal conditions in the wild, the scutes grow steadily as the tortoise uses calcium carbonate (from limestone), phosphorus (from green plants), and vitamin D (partly from wild plants and partly self-manufactured using sunlight) to form calcium phosphate, the substance bones are made from.

When a tortoise hibernates, its sources of calcium and phosphorus are abruptly removed and the margin of the scute becomes undercut. This produces a pattern on each scute. Raised rings represent annual growth and the grooves represent hibernation. The centre of each scute, which is unmarked with growth rings, is the size and shape that the scute was at the time of hatching. The "orange peel" surface of this area is an imprint of the inside of the egg shell. It should therefore be easy to age a tortoise. However, this idealised pattern can be broken up by a wide variety of events, which can make the interpretation of carapace ring patterns more difficult than it first appears and occasionally a real bone of contention.

In the wild, patterns (in *Testudo graeca)* generally are clear up until sexual

maturity at about five or six years of age, when changed behaviour patterns normally lead to one annual ring being broken up into mini-rings. Growth then continues reasonably regularly for many years. As the tortoise grows it needs more food each year and hence needs to control a bigger area. Eventually the position is reached, normally at about 20 years old, where the tortoise spends too much of its time walking round looking for food or chasing off intruding tortoises. Less time is spent eating, leading to the growth rate being considerably reduced. This effect controls the maximum size of tortoises in the wild. Please note that this control is affected by external influences and not by internal chemistry—this is significantly different from the more familiar mammalian system where size is controlled mainly by internal chemistry.

In captivity the situation becomes complicated by body heat deficiencies, dietary deficiencies, and behavioural and health problems caused by tortoises being kept together in too small an area. Careful observation and interpretation of the carapace ring patterns can assist considerably in trying to work out past husbandry shortcomings.

In general terms, when tortoises are moved from the wild to northern Europe the ring patterns change in four ways:

1) The hibernation grooves become less pronounced.

2) The width of the annual growth ring is approximately proportional to the number of hours per year that the tortoise can keep its body at 30°C (86°F). For tortoises kept in English gardens without artificial basking being available to them, this is dramatically less than the hours per year in the wild and results in a dramatic change of ring width on importation.

3) The annual rings become divided by mini-grooves caused by intermittent periods with insufficient basking facilities, illness, poor diet, or because calcium intake is mainly in the form of semi-soluble calcium carbonate rather than the soluble calcium bicarbonate form that is

obtained from plants in the wild.

4) The rings become undercut due to calcium deficiency.

These complications mean that although it is possible to estimate the age of imported tortoises it normally is not possible to be exact. It is possible, however, to form a reasonably clear picture of the tortoise's life history. One can normally pick out the age of sexual maturity, the age when imported, and sometimes even changes of ownership or moves by the owner. Good husbandry should aim at producing consistent, clear, annual rings.

The fact that tortoises can always grow has far-reaching effects in dealing with some disease problems. It should be realised that not only external features but also internal organs grow. This means that, for instance, if a disease destroys a large percentage of a human organ, it generally is not enough just to cure the disease, because the reduced function of the organ often will cause major problems or even death. However, if a tortoise suffers similar problems, provided that the disease can be cured and provided that sufficient function remains so that growth is possible, a new organ can grow

and its function can steadily improve.

There is another interesting side-effect of semi-adequate husbandry. In general, most tortoises imported were sexually mature because imported juveniles had a very poor life expectancy. I have, however, seen three surviving examples of males imported before sexual maturity that were very small because of previously described problems, but interestingly their tails had only developed to about half the normal length and their plastrons had not developed the usual concavity. All owners were told how to improve husbandry, but I do not know whether this will result in complete maleness arriving 30 years late!!

It should be clear from all the foregoing that "old" in tortoise terms is a comparative word and not the absolute that is implied in human terms. Tortoises die from accident, disease, malnutrition, and bad husbandry, but I have never, I repeat, never, seen a tortoise that died or was dying from old age. Hundred-year-old tortoises, properly cared for, are active, grow, and reproduce. A hundred years is not "old" in the human sense of being inevitably near death. It is likely that there is an upper age limit, but if there is, we are still a long way from knowing it.

Tortoises can always grow. This is nowhere more evident than on the reserve on Santa Cruz, Galapagos Island (Ecuador) where the Giants are protected and cared for. These animals can live for more than 100 years...and they keep growing and are active during this long period.

Geochelone elephantopus, the Galapagos Giant Tortoise, in captivity on the Galapagos Islands, Ecuador.

Above*: Augustus,* my pet *Testudo hermanni*, demonstrates his climbing ability. Yes, *Augustus* did manage to climb over this smooth, vertical wall which was 50% taller than he was!

Below: Two-month-old *Testudo graeca ibera* hatchlings munching on a piece of Sow Thistle. Both photos by the author.

THE SICK TORTOISE

This section is not intended to be a text book or even a complete listing of every problem that can affect tortoises. It is intended to be a guide for both tortoise owners and non-specialist vets to the diagnosis and treatment of common ailments that frequently are mishandled. If in any doubt, consult a veterinary surgeon who has studied reptile medicine. In the past this has been extremely difficult advice to follow as very few vets have studied reptiles. However, there are signs that the profession is trying to put this right. I hope that this book will tempt more vets to gain expertise in this fascinating subject.

ANOREXIA

Tortoise anorexia is, in my experience, the cause, either directly or indirectly, of the majority of adult tortoise deaths in England at the present time. It also is the potentially lethal complaint that is least understood by keepers, veterinary surgeons, and zoologists. These two statements probably explain each other.

Mammalian anorexia normally is either a mental condition or caused by vitamin deficiency. Vets who are not versed in reptilian medicine often will give a multivitamin injection or recommend keeping another tortoise for "company." Both of these actions, while appropriate for certain mammalian conditions, are at best ineffective and at worst very counterproductive when applied to tortoises.

Causes

The basic cause of tortoise anorexia is an abnormally high blood urea level. Urea is a by-product of animal body chemistry and normally is removed from the body by means of urination. Excess blood urea produces a variety of effects depending on concentration, but its primary effect is that of suppressing appetite.

Any disease can aggravate this condition, but the biggest problems are caused by mouth rot and nasal infections. Before attempting to treat anorexia, check carefully for any infections and treat as necessary.

Insufficient body temperatures will aggravate the problem. When a tortoise's body temperature is at 30°C (86°F) it gets hungry, and when it eats, its body is at the right temperature to process that food. When the body temperature drops, at night or in the daytime as hibernation approaches, the appetite drops with it. This is natural and normal. At night it produces sound sleep without pangs of hunger, and in late autumn it produces an empty gut ready for hibernation. Unfortunately, if the tortoise is out of doors during a cool spell in August or even a warm but cloudy spell the result is the same—anorexia. If this is the only problem, the cure is easy—provide a basking lamp and, if appropriate, some background heating.

High blood urea levels are caused by inadequate husbandry both in the summer and during hibernation. In ideal conditions, when a tortoise hibernates it slowly consumes body tissues and stores the resulting waste products (mainly uric acid compounds) in the kidneys. This process slowly increases the blood urea. When the tortoise wakes from hibernation, blood glucose levels are temporarily raised. This counteracts the effects of the high blood urea and provides energy for the tortoise to move, bask, and find food. As the tortoise eats and urinates, the blood urea and glucose levels return rapidly to their normal summer values.

Problems arise in a variety of ways if thermal husbandry is not correct. For example, if the tortoise is subject to a warm spell during hibernation sufficient to bring the body temperature up to 10°C (50°F), it will wake and the blood glucose system will operate. At nightfall the temperature falls and the tortoise goes back into hibernation. If this has happened in a box, the owner probably doesn't realise anything has happened. However, in the spring the glucose correction system is no longer adequate to correct the urea build-up and the result is anorexia.

The most common cause is spending long periods of hibernation with a body temperature three or four degrees above or below the optimum temperature. Under these circumstances the tortoise digs to correct its body temperature. In a box this has no effect, so the tortoise continues to dig, using body tissues as fuel and storing the resulting waste products in the kidneys. This can produce an enormous store of urates in the kidneys, resulting in blood urea levels a hundred times normal. The correction system that operates on waking only can deal with urea levels about ten times normal so this can cause severe anorexia.

It is relatively easy to prevent a Mediterranean tortoise from hibernating. However, if one does, one normally finds that during a cold or cloudy spell during the year the tortoise will stop eating and operate on the "closed cycle" for two or three weeks. When this happens urates are built up in the kidneys very rapidly because the tortoise is using a lot of energy.

If a tortoise is kept in a good thermal environment and on a good diet during the summer, it can succeed in shifting a lot of urates from the kidneys. If, however, it is kept inadequately it will succeed in moving very little. To avoid anorexia, good husbandry, both in the summer and in the winter, is necessary.

High urate levels, and hence anorexia, can result from one year's very bad hibernation or from a build-up of many years of "not quite good enough" hibernation and summer husbandry.

It is very important to realise that when a tortoise stops eating it burns body tissues for energy and stores the resulting urates in the kidneys, causing increased blood urea levels and more severe anorexia. This obviously is a downward spiral, and although it may take a long time, the final outcome is certain unless something is done to reverse the process.

The process of urate build-up accelerates considerably when the tortoise runs out of body fat. The utilisation of fat to provide energy is efficient. When the fat is used up the tortoise burns protein instead, and this is a much less efficient process, resulting in a rapid build-up of urates. A tortoise with low fat reserves

dies more rapidly from anorexia.

The quantity of waste products stored in the tortoise's kidneys can in extreme cases be unbelievable. In the most extreme case I have seen, the uric acid compounds, which normally are a creamy white fluid, had crystallised and looked rather like brown sugar when finally expelled. The kidneys were so enlarged from the crystals that a catheter would not pass beyond the throat into the stomach and a horizontal X-ray revealed that the swollen kidneys had pressed the lungs into a narrow strip below the carapace, making breathing very difficult. It sounds amazing, but that tortoise made a total recovery and is now living happily, but the treatment took a very long time.

Severity

In general terms, the severity of anorexia is dependent on the quantity of waste products stored in the kidneys and the depletion of the body tissues. These are generally, but not invariably, proportional.

The depletion of the body tissues can be checked by weighing the tortoise and by accurately (to within 1 mm) measuring the straight line carapace length between the nuchal scute and the supracaudal scute. Calculate the weight in grams divided by the length in centimetres cubed. This ratio is between 0.21 and 0.23 for a normal healthy adult. Malnutrition due to anorexia will reduce this ratio. Anything below 0.20 should be regarded as requiring attention. Below 0.18 should be regarded as urgent. Death occurs at about 0.15.

Depletion of body tissues is not the whole story. When anorexia is brought on by one bad hibernation suffered by an otherwise well-kept tortoise, body weight measurement provides a reasonably accurate guide to the severity of the anorexia. However, if the anorexia is caused by urates steadily built up year after year by semi-adequate husbandry, the tortoise will put back the depleted fat each summer and will be the same weight (at least temporarily) as a healthy tortoise. This kind of anorexia is harder to cure than the previous kind.

Above: *Geochelone elephantopus*, the Galapagos Giant Tortoise, in the wild on Galapagos. The hillside climate and vegetation preferred by these tortoises are very different from the hot, dry coastal climate of the Charles Darwin Station where the giant tortoises are kept in captivity.
Below: This *Testudo graeca* shows massive shell rot which has been left dirty and untreated for years, finally resulting in the animal's death. Both photos by the author.

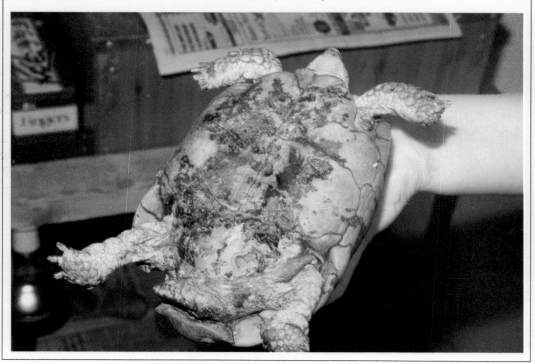

Above: Giant Seychelles tortoise from the Island of Fregate off the eastern coast of Africa.

Below: The courtship ritual of *Testudo graeca* begins.

The build-up of urates in the kidneys is not easy to quantify. If it is higher than normal then blood urea will be higher than normal and the blood glucose will be lower than normal, and these can be checked with a blood test. However, such tests are not easy to do because blood pressure is lower than in mammals and results are not always reliable because it is very easy to contaminate samples. I have found the best guide to be the behavioural changes that occur with varying severity.

When a tortoise is kept in less than adequate conditions, anorexia slowly builds up but the problem is generally unnoticed by its owner in the early stages. The following table gives a general idea of the progression of severity if steps are not taken to halt its advance.

Stage 1) The tortoise eats well but occasionally is fussy, only eating pre-ferred food (generally high protein and/or sweet food).

Stage 2) The tortoise eats reasonably but is fussy. Drinks within the first few weeks out of hibernation. Takes several days to start eating after hibernation.

Stage 3) The tortoise eats when the weather is hot but not when cloudy or cold. Drinks several times throughout the year. Takes weeks to start eating after hibernation. Loses weight.

Stage 4) The tortoise stops eating and passing water, urates, and faeces, but will bask normally if a lamp is provided. Loses weight. Can sometimes be hand-fed with persistence.

Stage 5) The tortoise does not eat or pass faeces, etc. Loses muscular strength. Tries to bask at a position where the temperature is exactly 30°C (86°F) rather than moving in and out of the warmest spots. Loses weight.

Stage 6) As 5), but the tortoise now avoids all heat and light, tries to hide and hibernate in coldest, darkest spot.

Stage 7) Comatose. Often mistaken for hibernation. This is only brief unless life is supported.

Every case of anorexia is different. Different tortoises react to incorrect thermal husbandry in different ways. The foregoing list is a guide, not a gospel.

Treatments

Various treatments have been sug-gested and tried over the years. The following is a discussion of all the meth-ods I have tried. The treatment necessary to get a tortoise back to normal behaviour patterns depends on the severity of the anorexia. In extreme cases treatment can take a very long time. One has to be patient and persevere. In extreme cases malnutrition can cause damage to internal organs, but although temporary damage is common, in my experience irreversible damage is rare.

When treating any case of anorexia, records are vital. Record weight at least daily and preferably before and after every action by either yourself or the tortoise. Record everything that is put into the tortoise, record any medication given, record everything that comes out of the tortoise, record thermal conditions, and record changes in the tortoise's capabili-ties and behaviour. If this is done, one can keep track of progress and if any problems occur it frequently is possible to work out what to do from the records.

Treatment No. 1

Provide the tortoise with adequate thermal conditions as described in previous chapters.

Comment: This removes the reason for the anorexia happening and the tortoise will get itself back to normal. This works for *Stage 1* and generally for *Stage 2*, but it is an insufficient remedy for more severe anorexia.

Treatment No. 2

Multivitamin injection.

Comment: Very widely used and **totally ineffective.**

Treatment No. 3

Stomach-tube the tortoise with a water and glucose solution once or twice.

Comment: This replicates the tortoise's own method of dealing with the problems of waking from hibernation. It can be miraculously effective in certain mild cases, particularly in cases where the W/L^3 (weight-length cubed) ratio is above .22 and the anorexia has been caused by only one bad hibernation. If this method proves ineffective within 48 hours there is no point in continuing. The method either works quickly or does not work at all.

Treatment No. 4

Keith Lawrence and Oliphant Jackson published the first attempts at an effective treatment in 1983. In principle this consists of:

a) maintaining body temperature at 25 to 30°C (77 to 86°F);

b) daily stomach-tubing with water plus Hartmann's solution;

c) weekly stomach tubing with Complan.

Comments: 1) The treatment is much more effective if the body temperature is 29 to 30°C (84 to 86°F). 2) Complan is a milk product. Since the publication of this method it has been demonstrated that long-term use of milk products is harmful. There are effective alternatives. 3) In severe cases where regrowth of body tissues is required, the recommended food input is sufficient to put off the date of death, but insufficient to cure the problem. This method is, however, generally effective on anorexia up to *Stage 4* severity and occasionally at *Stage 5*.

Treatment No. 5

This is basically refinements of and extensions to the method suggested by Lawrence and Jackson and can be used successfully in cases of any severity if common sense is used. In principle all one has to do is to keep the tortoise warm and feed it regularly.

1) Temperature—The tortoise's body temperature should be kept at 30°C (86°F) for 16 to 18 hours per day either by basking or, in more severe cases where the tortoise will not bask, by keeping it in a box with the air temperature thermostatically controlled at 30°C (86°F). In severe cases the tortoise will accept a 30°C (86°F) air temperature, but as progress is made the tortoise will struggle to be released. When this happens, the tortoise can be transferred to 25°C (77°F) air temperature with a 35°C (95°F) basking spot. Tortoises normally will accept one or the other. Check the tortoise's body temperature by putting a

hand on your own forehead and then on the tortoise's carapace. They should feel the same. The tortoise should not be allowed to get cooler than this. At night keep the tortoise in an air temperature of 20 to 25°C (68 to 77°F) and in insulation.

2) Feeding—The tortoise can be fed by stomach tube using any number of foods that can be liquefied and fed by using a syringe. There are a few practical difficulties. Food containing fibre, seeds, or skin can block the catheter, and this limits one's choice. For long-term health, low-protein, high-fibre vegetable matter is preferred, but for tube feeding, higher protein, lower fibre vegetable matter produces faster results. The water content is not critical, but I find that using just enough water to enable the syringe to be filled without clogging is about the correct consistency. Food should be supplemented with minerals and vitamins added to the mix. If the treatment is short-term (less than four weeks), I normally do not add extra calcium because I am trying to restore the soft parts of the body, not the hard parts. Calcium, in the form of grated cuttlebone or limestone flour, can be fed this way provided it is ground fine enough to avoid blocking the catheter. This should be done in cases of extended treatment.

The quantity of food required by a healthy tortoise is in direct ratio to its weight, and the weight is in direct ratio to the cube of its length. An anorexic tortoise's weight changes from normal, so this becomes an inappropriate yardstick for calculating food requirements. I therefore use "length cubed" as a yardstick. If the tortoise is overfed, it regurgitates the food. If the tortoise is underfed, the progress toward health and normal behaviour is painfully slow or non-existent. I use a formula of L (cubed)/333 to make a first estimate of the weight of food per day, where L is the carapace length in centimetres and the answer is in grammes (or ml if liquefied). This is best fed in two doses, the first one hour after commencement of basking and again eight to ten hours later.

3) Bathing—Daily warm baths, while probably not essential, appear to be

A view of the plastron of the Greek Tortoise, *Testudo graeca*. Photo by Isabelle Francais with the assistance of Mr. Abbott.

A view of the plastron of Hermann's Tortoise, *Testudo hermanni*. Photo by Isabelle Francais with the assistance of Mr. Abbott.

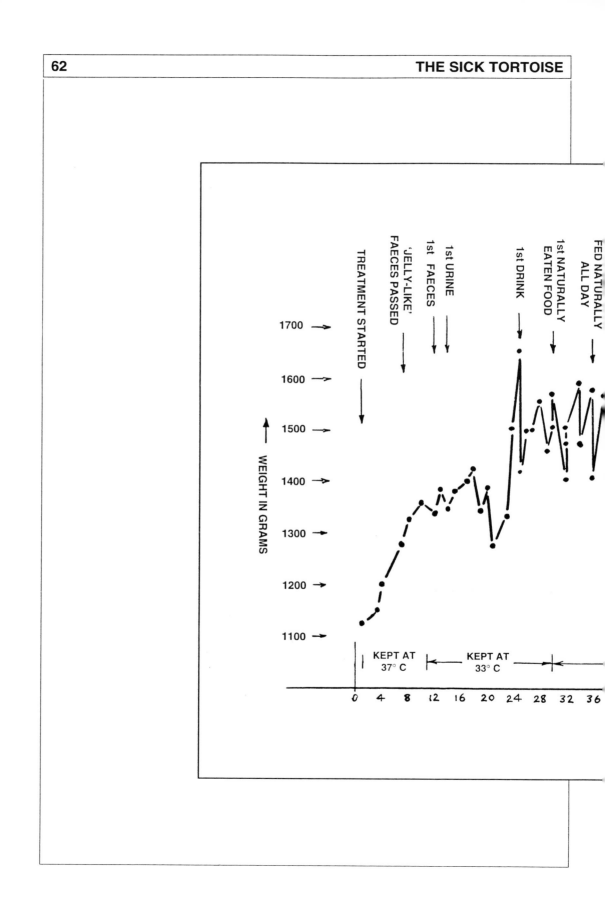

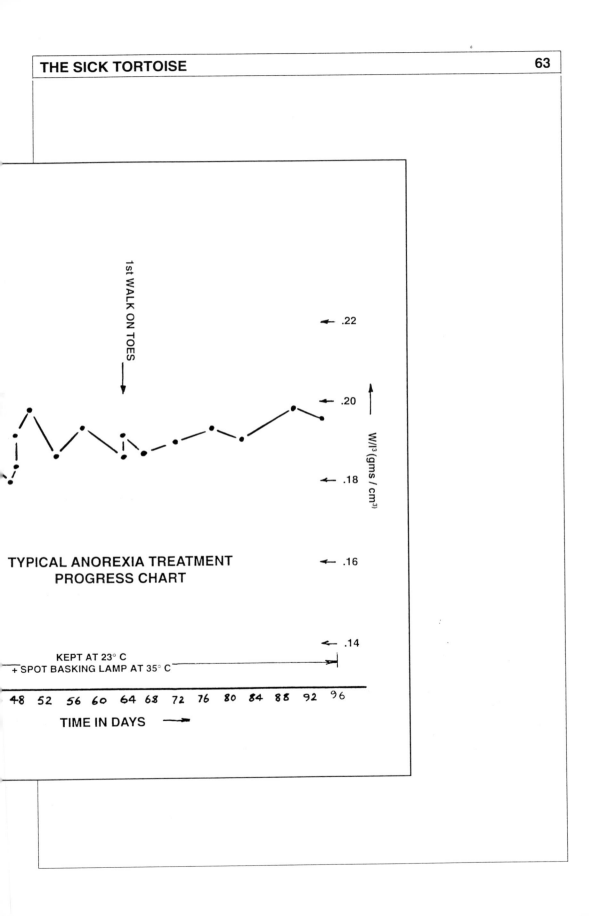

1st WALK ON TOES

.22

.20

W/l^3 (gms / cm³)

.18

**TYPICAL ANOREXIA TREATMENT
PROGRESS CHART**

.16

.14

KEPT AT 23° C
+ SPOT BASKING LAMP AT 35° C

48 52 56 60 64 68 72 76 80 84 88 92 96

TIME IN DAYS ⟶

*1) Testudo hermanni. 2) Geochelone chilensis. 3) Testudo graeca. 4) Testudo horsfieldi.
5) Geochelone elegans.* Photos by Burkhard Kahl.

beneficial, partly by getting the tortoise warmer and partly by encouraging the passage of waste products.

4) Drinking—Lawrence and Jackson suggested rehydrating by stomach-tube. I have found that in general this is not necessary, partly because one automatically introduces sufficient water when feeding and partly because the tortoise normally can be persuaded to do the job for itself if larger quantities are required. Offer the tortoise a drink from time to time. When anorexic, tortoises occasionally drink enormous quantities, partly to rehydrate their bodies but mainly to flush out the unwanted urates from their kidneys. Any drinking and subsequent urination comprise a highly beneficial step along the road to normality.

5) Weight Progress—It takes two to three weeks for food to pass from the tortoise's mouth to the vent. Untreated anorexic tortoises normally have an empty gut, therefore for the first two to three weeks the weight should go up by 10 gms for every 10 gms of food put in. After this, the weight will increase with input and reduce with output. The fluctuations can be very large at first, but should become less as the tortoise regains control over its water balance. After the first three weeks the average weight should increase at a slow but steady rate until the weight/length cubed ratio becomes normal.

6) Excretion Progress—Faeces are not produced until two to three weeks after starting feeding, sometimes sooner if the intestines were partly full. Sometimes a colourless, jelly-like substance is produced that is a waste product formed when body tissues are consumed. Very occasionally faeces come through slightly green indicating that digestion is incomplete. This happens sometimes with long-term untreated anorexics because, with no food in the gut, many of the naturally occurring microorganisms that normally assist with digestion die. Sometimes the faeces is too runny or too solid because of imperfect water control. These problems generally are short-term and self-correcting. Faeces steadily become more normal in appearance and frequency with continuing treatment.

Excretion of water can be very erratic, particularly in extreme cases, but steadily becomes more normal.

Excretion of uric acid compounds is the most important factor in assessing the progress of the treatment. Unfortunately, it is also the least predictable. Initially the waste products are slow to move, coming out in tiny quantities or only in solution in the excreted water. With continuing treatment, the waste products come out in larger than normal quantities of white creamy fluid. Often the kidneys initially fail to separate the water from the creamy fluid and it comes out mixed. With continuing treatment, the separation improves and quantities return to normal.

In extreme cases, the uric acid compounds are tightly compressed in the kidneys, changing the compounds from white to yellow, then brown, and from a creamy consistency to a thick consistency, finally crystallising like brown sugar. In these cases the treatment becomes very prolonged (up to two years!), but observation of excretion patterns should reveal steady progress down the road to normality.

7) Physical Progress—After an extended period of untreated anorexia a tortoise becomes virtually inert. Generally the decline is very slow and steady and many owners don't seem to notice until it is well-advanced. Some individuals, particularly males, in spite of steadily losing weight, remain very active and alert. In these cases they become inert fairly dramatically. In this inert condition they lose all muscle power, can no longer stand, collapse onto their plastrons, and have trouble lifting their heads. What is less obvious is that the muscles controlling bladder function plus the muscles that push food through the gut also cease to function efficiently. As treatment progresses, all these functions slowly return.

Timing

It should be obvious to anyone reading this chapter that the first signs of anorexia normally show themselves in the spring when a tortoise wakes from hibernation. If this is dealt with immediately, even in extreme cases it normally is possible to effect a complete cure before hibernation time. Unfortunately, many owners delay a considerable time before seeking help, hoping that things will get better. Even more unfortunately, other owners have tried to get help and found the help inadequate. This can lead to a situation where treatment starts late in the year, with the result that the arrival of winter interferes with the treatment.

If appropriate, the onset of hibernation can be delayed by keeping the tortoise in artificial summer conditions (25°C [77°F] air temperature, 35°C [95°F] basking temperature, 14+ hours of daylight).

It is possible to totally prevent hibernation by this method, but this can produce future anorexia because the tortoise frequently reacts by going into the "closed cycle" at some time during the following year. Therefore I recommend that if it is necessary to extend the treatment over the winter, one hibernates the tortoise normally, but for a shortened period (one or two months) and takes great care to control hibernation temperature very accurately to avoid making the anorexia worse. Under these circumstances it is important to keep the "shutting down" period short (about three weeks) and to get the tortoise's body temperature up to 30°C (86°F) as soon as possible after hibernation (preferably within 24 hours).

Important Points

1) If a tortoise shows *any* signs of mild anorexia it is a sign of incorrect husbandry. The husbandry should be put right immediately.

2) If a tortoise stops eating, *do something about it immediately.* If you don't, it normally gets steadily worse, not better.

3) If you are tube-feeding and you want to try to wean the tortoise onto feeding for itself, the best time to offer food is immediately after tube-feeding. I know this is counter to one's intuition, but it is true! Do not starve the tortoise to try to give it an appetite; it just doesn't work for anorexic tortoises!

4) Be prepared for the long haul. You must not expect to correct years of

incorrect husbandry in five minutes. It normally takes about the same length of time to cure as the time the tortoise has spent being anorexic, and if there are complications it can take twice as long. But never despair. With care, perseverence, careful observation, and common sense, it is amazing what can be achieved. Our success rate has been about 98%.

TUBE-FEEDING

If a tortoise is mildly anorexic, one can feed it by forcibly opening its mouth and touching the tongue with food. The tortoise then will eat that food and, with luck, the whole leaf if one is skillful in putting in a new piece just as the mouth is opened to get rid of the last piece. This method can be a useful short-term expedient but it is extremely time consuming. Also, some tortoises become distressed by repetitive forcible mouth opening, and the method simply will not work with severe anorexia. The alternative is to use a stomach-tube. This method also is the appropriate one for administering certain medications, in particular medication for controlling internal parasites.

Many owners show great reluctance to attempt tube-feeding, but it is not a difficult process provided one is willing to exercise care and to persevere. What is more important is that if it is done skillfully the tortoise appears to suffer no distress whatsoever. I have even known some patients undergoing long-term treatment that would open their own mouths when presented with a catheter! I feel that caring owners should learn to use this technique—it can save lives and, at the very least, will mean that it is easier to keep your pets free of internal parasites.

Method

This is easiest with two people. Cut a standard dog catheter plastic tube obtainable from veterinary suppliers to a length to suit the tortoise. Fit the catheter and syringe together. It is easier to use a syringe that is the correct size for the quantity you are administering. Clean both the catheter and syringe thoroughly inside and out. Fill the syringe.

Sit in a chair, preferably in a position that no one can walk in front of and disturb the tortoise. Put an old towel across your knees to prevent mess. Place the tortoise on your lap with its tail and back legs between your legs, with the head facing your right hand and with the body at a 45° angle to the floor. In this position you can control the position of the tortoise using only your legs, leaving both hands free. Also, this position normally causes the tortoise to stretch out the front legs and head for balance, saving you the effort of pulling the head out.

Place the thumb and first finger of your left hand behind the back of the tortoise's skull and allow the tortoise to trap them between the skull and the front of its carapace. If your tortoise has a fold of skin on its neck, carefully push the fold back to avoid trapping it. It is important to move one's fingers very slowly. Don't jerk if the tortoise moves; tortoises are frightened by sudden movements.

Pull down the lower jaw using the thumb and first finger of your right hand. Generally this is not difficult, but there are two circumstances where some skill and strength are required. First, if the tortoise has not opened his mouth for 12 months the jaws can be glued together with solidified saliva. You normally can overcome this by using your fingernails as levers in the gap between the jaws. Second, a large, warm, healthy tortoise that requires routine de-worming can be a handful. It will use the front claws and leg scales to try to force your grip. Use the third and fourth fingers of each hand to pin his legs back.

The assistant now inserts the catheter along the roof of the tortoise's mouth and steadily slides it in full length. It should slide in smoothly with no resistance. Steadily press the plunger to empty the syringe and then steadily withdraw the catheter. The whole process should only take about ten seconds. If the process is carried out efficiently, the tortoise accepts it with good grace. If one takes too long, the tortoise fights and the process be-

comes more difficult.

It is perfectly possible to do this single-handed, but this does require some dexterity so I would recommend that one practises doing it using two people first. When stomach-tubing single-handed, use the thumb and second finger of your left hand to support the back of the tortoise's skull. Open the mouth with your right hand, then put the tip of your left hand first finger in the mouth, holding it open and leaving your right hand free to operate the syringe—not so easy if your tortoise decides to fight!!

ACCIDENTS

One frequently sees adult tortoises with carapace damage that obviously is the result of broken bones that subsequently have healed. Although this clearly can be the result of an accident happening in the home, the large majority of the cases I have examined are due to "collection damage." When the tortoises were collected from the wild, collectors would look for disturbed earth and then use a spade to dig up buried tortoises. Inaccurate spade blows produced the inevitable results.

Natural recovery from such accidents is dependent on a series of factors:

1) The severity of the original injury.

2) Cleanliness. The cleaner the wound, the less the chance of infection.

3) State of health. The more efficient the tortoise's immune system, the better the chances of recovery from subsequent infections.

4) Body temperature. Healing is very much retarded if the tortoise's body temperature is less than 30°C (86°F).

5) Diet. New flesh and bone will not grow adequately without adequate raw material. In particular, carapace damage will not repair unless adequate amounts of calcium are fed.

Accident Prevention

A few tips to help avoid accidents follow.

1) Make sure all tortoises are safely locked away before using garden machinery, setting bonfires, or moving compost heaps. Just one small mistake can have

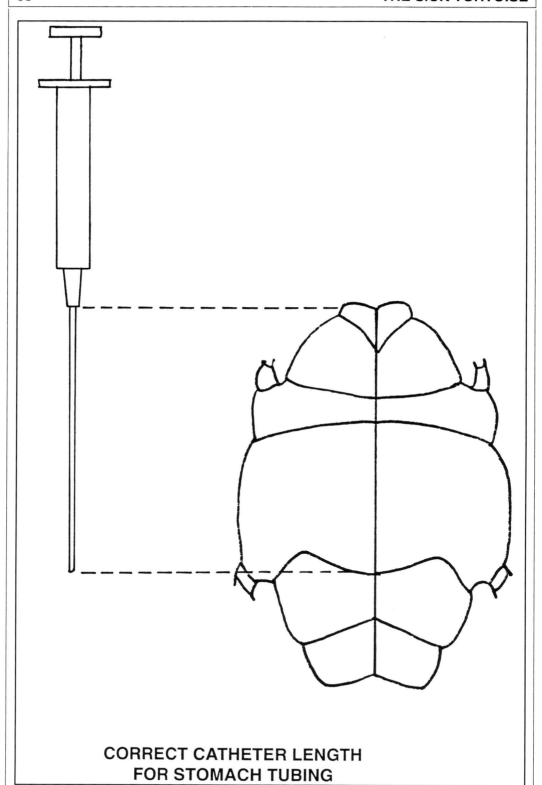

**CORRECT CATHETER LENGTH
FOR STOMACH TUBING**

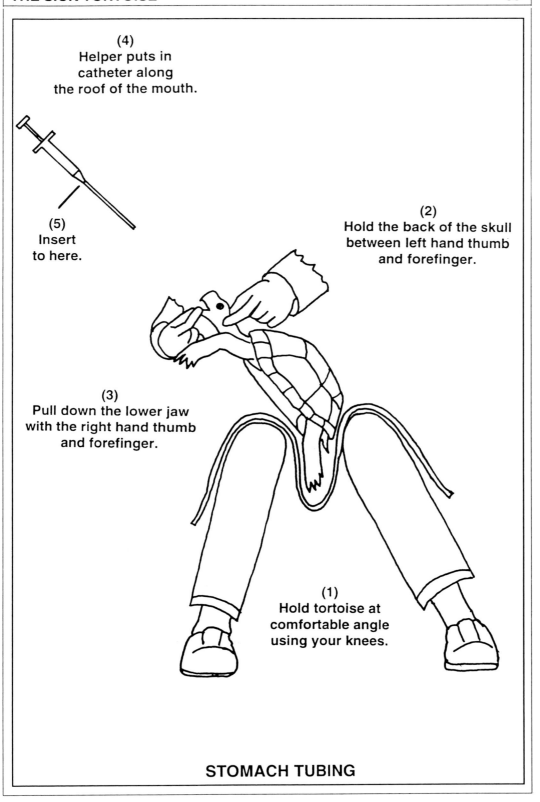

(4)
Helper puts in
catheter along
the roof of the mouth.

(5)
Insert
to here.

(2)
Hold the back of the skull
between left hand thumb
and forefinger.

(3)
Pull down the lower jaw
with the right hand thumb
and forefinger.

(1)
Hold tortoise at
comfortable angle
using your knees.

STOMACH TUBING

horrific consequences.

2) Be careful when gardening, especially using garden forks.

3) Healthy tortoises like to climb, but having ascended they descend by sliding or falling. Do not, therefore, have paved or concreted areas beneath rockeries or steps. Do not use plants such as clematis against outside walls.

4) Make sure that tortoises have no possible access to garden ponds. If the worst happens, try to empty the lungs of water by holding the tortoise in a head down position and moving its front legs slowly in and out. Then leave it in a warm position to recover. If a tortoise falls into cold water, the thermal shock considerably slows the breathing and heartbeat. Drowning, therefore, takes longer for tortoises than with mammals, often hours rather than minutes, but death is just as sure unless reasonably prompt action is taken.

5) Do not hibernate tortoises on a shelf above a concrete floor. This spells disaster if the tortoise wakes and climbs out.

6) Do not allow tortoises access to any road or building used by motor vehicles.

Accident Treatment

There are no basic differences in the ways of treating accidental wounds, cuts, and broken bones between tortoises and mammals. Minor cuts should be cleaned, treated with an antiseptic cream and covered exactly as one would treat a similar human cut. Plasters can be helpful in keeping out dirt.

Broken limb bones can be set and splinted exactly like mammalian bones. Unfortunately, there has been a veterinary tendency not to attempt this but to instead to such gimmicks as castors glued to the plastron, so the unsplinted leg heals in a deformed shape. A castor is only of marginal help to a limbless tortoise indoors and is a positive hindrance outdoors.

Broken carapaces and plastrons have, in the past, normally been repaired by veterinary surgeons using "car body" techniques. Covering damaged carapaces with epoxy resin is an invitation for shell rot and other diseases to form underneath. Epoxy resin in a carapace crack makes the correct healing of that crack virtually impossible. Examination of such repairs shows subsequent infection in a majority of cases after five years and incomplete healing in a significant minority of cases.

In most cases, broken carapaces are able to be set and splinted. This method of repair obviously will take the veterinary surgeon much more time and trouble and hence will cost more than "car body" techniques, but the result should be a permanent rather than a temporary repair.

A good repair using epoxy resin is possible but requires considerable expertise. Extreme care must be taken to ensure that any area subsequently covered by resin is surgically clean. This is not easy. Any shell rot must be cured before covering the shell with resin; if it isn't, the rot will grow under the resin. Veterinary resin (developed for repairing horse hooves) should be used. Cracks should be filled with antibiotic cream and/or absorbable gauze so that resin does not get into the crack and make healing impossible. The repair should be checked (preferably by a veterinary surgeon) for subsequent infection from time to time.

Any veterinary work is only half the job. It is essential to keep the tortoise healthy, warm, well-fed, and on a calcium-rich diet if healing is to take place. It is important to realise that no healing of bone or carapace fractures is possible during hibernation because the mechanism of calcium utilisation is temporarily halted. Under these circumstances I would recommend only a very short (say two weeks) hibernation and ensure that the tortoise otherwise is kept in optimal summer conditions.

Dogs

In general, dogs ignore tortoises. However, I regularly see a small but significant number of damaged tortoises with tell-tale tooth marks on their carapaces. Cross-questioning owners reveals a pattern. Every owner claims they have never seen it happen. Every owner tells me "My dog wouldn't do that."

Dogs's instincts are those of carnivorous pack hunters. When domesticated, their human owners become their pack leaders. When the pack leader is present, he organises their hunting and their food. When he is not present, the dog will set about organising his own hunting and food, and that could well mean the pet tortoise.

In my opinion, dogs and tortoises should not be kept together. If for some reason it is necessary to have tortoises and dogs in the same household, they should *never* be left alone together. Would you leave your child unattended in a tiger's cage? Do you believe that arguments that it is a nice tiger, that it is well-fed, or that it has never eaten anyone before are very convincing?

GENERAL HEALTH

Before describing diseases it is necessary to describe what a healthy tortoise looks like. During the day during the summer, the tortoise should be warm to the touch. It should be able to stand and walk rapidly on the tips of the claws with the plastron well clear of the ground. When undisturbed, the tortoise should demonstrate exploratory behaviour, sniffing around any new area. When aware of possible danger, it should "freeze" with the neck outstretched, the nostrils held high, and with the skin under the jaw fluctuating to check the smells in the air.

When picked up, the tortoise should express displeasure with a hiss and should fight to be released. If a tortoise does not behave in this way, then something is wrong. It may be suffering from a disease, some internal damage, a dietary deficiency, or may simply not be being kept properly.

HYGIENIC ISOLATION

If you own a group of tortoises and one becomes ill with an infectious or contagious disease, it is important to stop the problem from passing to others in the group. This is done by separating the healthy animals from the sick ones. Most owners are not very good at this. They put

a stop to some methods of transmission but not all, and unfortunately one chink in the armour can all too often be one chink too many.

Be prepared—think ahead. If one of your tortoises becomes sick how can you separate it? If several become sick, can you separate the healthy ones? Indoors and outdoors? If several become sick and are cured one at a time, can you handle convalescence to avoid re-infection? If males and females are sick can you still separate them if necessary?

As well as permanent isolation areas, I keep a stock of "Thermalite building blocks" that can be used at five minute's notice to build any appropriate isolation compound. It is helpful to be able to differentiate between infectious and non-infectious problems, but if in doubt, assume any problem is infectious.

1) Do not leave a healthy and an infected tortoise together a minute longer than necessary.

2) Remove and burn all bedding and floor covering as often as possible.

3) Avoid faeces or urine coming in contact with food.

4) When carrying out daily chores, deal with healthy animals first then the sick.

5) Keep food separate. In particular, do not give food uneaten by sick tortoises to healthy tortoises.

6) Do not walk from a "sick" area into a "healthy" area.

7) Wash your hands thoroughly after handling sick tortoises.

8) Thoroughly scrub and disinfect any area that has been used by a sick tortoise before putting any other tortoise in that area.

9) Thoroughly scrub and disinfect all areas as often as possible and on a routine basis.

Bacteria and viruses cannot be seen, but one must be aware of their presence and act accordingly. Prevention of disease is always better than cure.

DEATH

I have seen cases of tortoises diagnosed as dead that were not dead. I know that this sounds odd, but it is true. When ill and/or cold a tortoise's heartbeat, breathing, and other bodily functions can slow down dramatically and it is easy to be fooled into thinking they have totally stopped. One owner dropped in to see me while on his way to dispose of a tortoise that he decided had died; this diagnosis had just been confirmed by his local vet. The tortoise is now cured, fit, and healthy.

The problem was that the tortoise had been suffering from a severe infection. The owner took him to a local vet who correctly injected antibiotic doses sufficient to cure the problem, but unfortunately picked an antibiotic to which this particular animal showed an allergic reaction. The result was a drug-induced coma that incorrectly was diagnosed as death. The owner now thinks I can walk on water, having brought his pet back from the dead, but in fact all I did was to keep the tortoise's body temperature at 30°C (86°F) for a week, waiting for the effects of the drug to wear off, and then I carried out life support as if treating for anorexia.

The way to check if a tortoise is really dead is to put him under a basking lamp for about 15 to 30 minutes. If the heart is still beating, the whole of the body will become evenly warm; if the tortoise is dead the carapace will become scorching hot and the limbs will remain cold.

If a tortoise dies from an infection, the cadaver will contain a high concentration of infectious bacteria and should be disposed of either by burning or by deep burial as soon as possible after the event. Keep it away from other tortoises, humans, and food. Thoroughly disinfect any areas with which the diseased animal had contact. Thoroughly wash yourself and your clothes after handling the corpse. If you have other tortoises, promptly take them to a vet for examination.

Ten years ago, almost every affliction that attacked tortoises was considered incurable. Since then, great strides have been made in the understanding and treatment of all the common ailments.

OSTEODYSTROPHY

This is extremely common. 99%of

captive tortoises exhibit symptoms of osteodystrophy, some mild, some very severe. This is caused by lack of calcium in the diet. It is theoretically possible for it to be due to other causes (lack of phosphorus, vitamin D, or sunlight), but in every case I have seen, increasing the daily input of calcium carbonate to about 50% of the diet by weight improves the situation immeasurably. Altering other factors seems to make no measurable difference. In extreme cases tortoises can be fed a diet consisting of 60 to 70% calcium carbonate and 30 to 40% vegetable matter for a short period to effect rapid improvement without any apparent side effects. Please note that the percentages quoted are not mistakes! I find it very difficult to persuade some owners to feed enough calcium!

SHELL ROT

This is a very common problem; about 75% of captive tortoises exhibit some symptoms. It is almost universally unrecognised by owners and vets alike.

The outer surface of the carapace and plastron consists of a series of layers. The outer layer is a hard material similar to human fingernails; next is a soft shock-absorbing layer, then a hard bony layer. If the outer layer suffers minor damage, provided that the area is clean and the tortoise warm, growing, and has a calcium-rich diet, the damage heals and the scar is minimal. However, if the tortoise is cold, not growing, calcium-deficient, and never washed, bacteria enter the wound and eat away the soft, shock-absorbing layer. The organisms that do this generally are anaerobic; that is, they prefer oxygen-deficient conditions. Carapaces subsequently covered in oil or dirt provide ideal conditions for the bacteria by protecting them from oxygen-rich air.

A minor infection of shell rot can be recognised by a lighter coloured surface surrounding mechanical damage. The colour change is due to the undercut top layer. Although it can occur anywhere on the carapace or plastron, the rear end of a female's carapace is a very common site. If the damage is untreated, it gets steadily worse and can remove the whole of the outside of the carapace. It also can extend deeper into the underlying bones, opening the way for other infections and becoming very ugly indeed.

Prevention

It is difficult to believe with such a potentially nasty complaint that prevention is easy, but it is! Keep your tortoise clean, then it can never happen! Do not use oil! Wash tortoises regularly. Soap and water normally will suffice, but detergent is necessary if oil has been used mistakenly.

Cure

Break back the affected areas and scrub them with a surgical scrubbing solution, using a toothbrush or nailbrush. In order to avoid splashing the tortoise's eyes, put a folded towel over his head. Scrub daily for one or two weeks, then weekly. This will kill the bacteria. Make sure the tortoise is warm, growing, and on a calcium-rich diet. This will heal the wounds, provided the underlying bone is not severely damaged. In any event, this treatment will effect a large improvement. Healing can take a long time in severe cases, so be patient and keep trying.

If the infection is extensive, has affected the bony layer, or is bleeding, antibiotics given by injection or as a cream may be required. See a vet specialising in reptiles.

INFECTIONS

When they are warm, clean, and fed on a good diet, tortoises have an efficient immune system, so infection problems are virtually non-existent. If an infection occurs, for example through a dirty wound, the treatment is the same as for a mammal (i.e., clean and disinfect the wound, inject with an antibiotic if necessary). The effectiveness of the treatment, however, is very dependent on good husbandry. The tortoise subsequently must be kept clean, warm, and on a good diet or else the recovery rate will be slow or even non-existent.

In general, injections should be given in the lower forelimb. This is because blood from the rear limbs passes directly through the kidneys, where the antibiotics are partially filtered out. The antibiotics that are the most efficacious with tortoises are associated with some degree of kidney toxicity. Side effects are often worse with anorexic tortoises.

ABSCESSES

A localised infection left untreated for many years will sometimes become an abscess. The most common site for this to happen is in the ear, but they can occur in a wide variety of places. Many owners seem not to notice, but an asymmetrical swelling on the side of the head is clear even on cursory inspection. Abscesses should be surgically removed. If left untreated, abscesses slowly grow until the infection swamps the tortoise's immune system. Death will follow rapidly from septicaemia (blood poisoning).

INTERNAL PARASITES (WORMS)

All tortoises suffer from worms and should be dewormed from time to time. How often deworming is required depends on the way the tortoises are kept. In particular, more frequent treatment will be required if:

1) tortoises are kept in groups; the larger the group the more often treatment is required;

2) tortoises are kept is small areas; the smaller the area the more often treatment is required;

3) tortoise quarters are cleaned out infrequently; when faeces and urine come into contact with food, internal parasites pass from infected to uninfected animals;

4) when tortoises are not eating well; when faeces are not passed regularly, worm eggs have more time to hatch and the infestation can rapidly expand.

I recommend that all tortoises be dewormed at intervals of one year (for groups of tortoises kept "zoo fashion") and three years (for solitary tortoises in first-class health kept in large clean areas). The scale of infestation can be judged in an individual case by taking a faeces sample to your vet so that it can be microscopically examined for worm eggs. Microscopic examination is considerably more reliable if carried out within 24 hours of the sample being passed, so make arrangements with your vet before you take a sample.

Dosing is done by stomach-tube. The traditional method is to dose twice at three to four week intervals. This is because the preparations kill the worms but are not 100% lethal to their eggs. The second dose is given to kill the worms newly hatched in the period between doses. The modern method is to dose once using more effective preparations. I have found the traditional method keeps the tortoises free of worms for longer periods, but either method is acceptable.

If you have a large group of tortoises, it is worth learning how to deworm and do it yourself. However, be warned—do it under veterinary supervision. *Do not* use compounds intended for cats and dogs—they can be lethal. Use accurately measured dose rates. The most effective drug available at the time of writing is oxfendazole ("Synanthic").

Most internal parasites can be effectively dealt with in this way. The major exceptions are flagellates.

INTERNAL PARASITES (FLAGELLATES)

Worms do not appear to cause the tortoise much discomfort until the infestation becomes very large, and even then the tortoise seems to be able to live with them provided it is in otherwise good health. Flagellates are different. They are small, invisible to the naked eye, and are potentially lethal. Most internal parasites consume the bowel contents, but flagellates destroy the intestinal wall. Once this is gone the tortoise can no longer process its food, and death is inevitable.

The symptoms of flagellates are a rapid reduction of appetite and the faeces becoming dark and runny. If this happens, a faeces sample immediately should be checked under a microscope. A few flagellates are present in normal faeces, but in these circumstances large numbers are present.

Treatment should be carried out without further delay. Any delay means more internal damage and compounds the problems. Separate any infected animals. Carry out isolation procedures,

paying extreme attention to food and waste products. You can use a stomach-tube with "Flagyl S," but unfortunately this kills not only the flagellates, but also the benign intestinal microorganisms that assist food digestion. This means that although the infestation normally is cured with one dose, the tortoise frequently can no longer digest its food and has no appetite. If the tortoise does not eat, or does not eat much, tube-feed the animal. If digestion is not occurring correctly, the tortoise continues to pass diarrhoea, but this generally will be lighter in colour. If the damage done by the flagellates was extensive, the faeces will come out the same colour that it went in—green. In this case, about 5 ml of *live* (i.e., not pasteurised) natural yogurt tube-fed in addition to the food will re-introduce appropriate benign microorganisms. One dose is sufficient. Be very hygienic and avoid contact with any other diseases during convalescence. The immune system does not appear to operate well at this time, and subsequent infectious problems are common.

Prevention

Flagellates occur naturally in the intestines of all tortoises, but their numbers normally are kept in check. Problems occur only when they proliferate. This happens when warm, healthy, hungry tortoises are kept in too small an area with inadequate hygiene and thus are forced to consume food contaminated with urine and faeces. It has been suggested to me that tortoises should be kept at less than optimum body temperatures in order to avoid this problem because they are then much less hungry and do not eat contaminated food. However, I feel that although this obviously works, one is only replacing one problem with other problems and it cannot be right to aim at less than 100% fitness. The right solution must be better hygiene and more area per tortoise.

RUNNY NOSE SYNDROME (RNS)

This is a common nasal tract infection. The symptoms are a clear, watery discharge from the nostrils, sometimes in the form of bubbles, and occasional sneezing. If untreated, sometimes it clears up, sometimes it recurs, and sometimes it progresses to infect the respiratory tract and finally the lungs (i.e., it becomes pneumonia). If the disease does spread to the respiratory tract, breathing becomes audible and, finally, noisy.

Until recently this was considered incurable and caused the deaths of many tortoises (death finally occurring as a result of pneumonia). It has been variously suggested that the source of the problem might be humidity, temperature, pollen, or dust. This was because the problem reappeared after workers thought they had cured it and because in its early stages it is virtually unaffected by large doses of injected antibiotics. This view was reinforced by the fact that several workers tried to isolate possible infection agents by taking swabs of the discharge and culturing the microorganisms found, but without success.

It is now clear that RNS is an extremely infectious disease. The reappearance of symptoms is due to reinfection from the surroundings. At the time of writing, the details of which agents are responsible for this condition and of how the disease operates are still uncertain. However, effective methods of treatment now have been established. The reason injections are ineffective probably is that the offending microorganisms occur in the mucus and hence have very little direct connection with the bloodstream.

Once one understands what is happening, the cure is relatively straightforward. Squirt a small quantity of a dilute general antibiotic (e.g., framomycin) up the nostrils using a small syringe and catheter. Repeat three or four times per day for seven days (or for two days after all symptoms have stopped). It also is possible to administer this medication by holding the tortoise's head out, opening the mouth, squirting the antibiotic into the mouth, and simultaneously releasing the head so that the withdrawal of the head into the carapace forces the contents of the mouth down the nostrils. It's easier than it sounds, but it does require

good timing. Occasionally the microorganisms prove resistant and it is necessary to use an alternative antibiotic. In general, however, the antibiotic and its concentration appear unimportant. Trials by O. Jackson and others indicate that it is the cleaning and flushing action that produces the majority of the effective treatment.

This, however, is only half the cure. Unless one takes extremely stringent precautions, the tortoise will become reinfected from it surroundings. Continue to use stringent hygiene for at least another two weeks after all symptoms have disappeared. Once you have the bugs on your premises it requires a lot of hard work and disinfecting to get rid of them!

PNEUMONIA

Pneumonia is an infection in the lungs. Its symptoms are lethargy, lack of appetite, and laboured noisy breathing. It is lethal. Every case I have seen has followed either RNS or some other debilitating disease.

It can be cured by an appropriate course of antibiotic injections. If your tortoise develops noisy breathing, take it to a vet right away.

MOUTH INFECTIONS

The mouths of tortoises should be examined if any disease is suspected and also on a routine basis. The inside of the mouth is covered with naked mucous membrane. The shapes of a tortoise's mouth and tongue differ from those of a human, but the coloration and texture should be similar.

A tortoise's pulse rate is dependent upon body temperature. When the body temperature is 30° (86°F), the tongue and mouth should be a bright, healthy pink. When a tortoise is cold the blood circulation is slow and the mouth appears "jaundiced," i.e., it is parchment-coloured around the margins, spreading to the centre of the tongue in extreme cases.

If the mouth is jaundiced when the tortoise is warm, something is wrong. A large number of diseases and deficiency problems can show this effect. Look carefully for other symptoms and carefully review your husbandry techniques and diet. If in doubt, take your tortoise to a specialist vet.

Any problem in the mouth, even a minor one, will cause a loss of appetite and hence trigger secondary problems of anorexia and malnutrition if not treated. If any problem occurs have it attended to promptly.

The possibility of mouth infections is made more likely by tube-feeding, partly because a tortoise's immune system is less effective at the time and partly because one can introduce germs while administering food. Be vigilant.

A common throat infection shows itself as sticky saliva that spills over the lower jaw making it slippery, and if the mouth is opened the saliva "strings" across the mouth. This is fairly easy to cure. Swab the mouth twice a day with a dilute antiseptic and continue for two days after the symptoms have disappeared. Antiseptics that do not wash away quickly are obviously more effective. Use framomycin in ointment form or betadine. If untreated, this infection can spread to the eyes and ears and eventually to the lungs, becoming pneumonia.

Mouth Rot

Mouth rot is a general term for a variety of fungal, bacterial, and viral mouth ailments. The appearance of the mouth differs according to the cause and the severity of the infection, but if one looks into the tortoise's mouth, the fact that there is an infection is generally clear even to an inexperienced owner. All forms of mouth rot are potentially lethal, but all will respond to appropriate topical treatment. The problem here is diagnosing the cause and hence finding the right treatment. There is no alternative but to go to a vet who is experienced in reptile medicine.

EYES

There are two reasons for eye damage—frost and infection. Healthy eyes are smooth, spherical, and look like shiny black glass. The surroundings of infected eyes normally swell, partly or totally closing them, and there often is a discharge.

Frost damage normally shows as small areas of partial light discolouration on or in the surface of the eyes. The way to check for this, if you do not have the luxury of optical instruments, is to stand out of doors with your back to the sun and hold the tortoise up in front of you so that the sun shines in its eyes. Small surface imperfections then will be visible.

When a tortoise cannot see properly, it has trouble finding its food and often becomes disoriented, walking in tight circles apparently chasing the only remaining spot of light it can see through one eye. This disorientation sometimes has been misdiagnosed as a mental problem. (Although mental problems are obviously possible, I have yet to find a "mental" problem that on investigation did not turn out to be something else.)

Eye infections can, in general, be effectively treated using the same products and methods as those used for mammals. If treated early, the cure should be total. However, long-term infection can cause damage that persists after the infection has been cured. Amazingly, tortoises can so something that humans can't. Provided that they are in good general health, are warm and growing, and their diet is rich in vitamin A, their damaged eyes will regrow! This applies both to frost- and infection-damaged eyes.

The most easily available source of vitamin A may be one of several vitamin mixtures intended for children. These mixtures usually are liquids and can be fed by putting a drop or two on the food. One word of warning, however: it is possible to overdose with vitamin A, so use the supplement as a substitute for, not in addition to, the multivitamin mix recommended for normal use.

Partial blindness sometimes can be totally cured and total blindness can sometimes be made only partial. A total cure of total blindness normally is not possible. However, some sight improvement plus teaching the tortoise to rely more on its sense of smell can make a dramatic difference in the capabilities of the tortoise and is well worth trying for. If the original problem was caused by frost, do something about your hibernation techniques. Don't make it worse.

When feeding blind or partially sighted tortoises, rather than feeding them totally by hand, try putting food in a large white bowl propped up at about 45°. This keeps the food and its smell concentrated in an area that is easy to find. Always feed in exactly the same place. Many tortoises will learn to feed themselves even when blind.

PREGNANCY PROBLEMS

A careful reading of the chapter on breeding should convince a tortoise keeper that it is perfectly possible for a female tortoise to have eggs inside her even if she hasn't seen a male for many years. It also should convince one of the dangers of keeping male and female tortoises together without taking the trouble to arrange egglaying facilities.

The only way of being sure a female remains egg-free (if that is what you wish to do) is to ensure that she *never* comes into contact with any males, *and* to remove *all* eggs from previous matings. Get her X-rayed, preferably in late spring or early summer, and if there are eggs inside her, have laying induced. Repeat these precautions the following year and continue until the tortoise has not produced any eggs for three years. Yes, this is a lot of trouble, and five or six years of perseverance will be negated in two minutes by a healthy male if he is given half a chance!

If a female is kept—as most northern European owners keep them—with fully formed eggs inside her, the eggs are basically inert and generally cause no problems, except for a reduced appetite. Occasionally, if the female attempts to expel these overcalcified eggs or if an egg becomes diseased, the results can be sudden, dramatic, and lethal. In many cases the choice is not between prevention and cure, but between prevention and death.

If the back legs of an apparently healthy female tortoise suddenly become unable to support her rear end and the tortoise shows signs of distress, get her to a specialist vet immediately. Do not waste a minute, and keep your fingers crossed. Generally in these circumstances immediate specialist treatment is essential for survival.

Problems commonly arise when pregnant females are kept on calcium-deficient (or less commonly vitamin-deficient) diets. In these circumstances either the female tries to lay the eggs but the contractions fail to expel them, or the eggs are laid without shells, normally singly and without the female digging a nest. Sometimes the eggs come out whole and sometimes they are "scrambled" and mixed with urine or faeces. The solution is straightforward—increase dietary calcium. This can be done rapidly if necessary by stomach-tubing with a mixture of food and limestone flour, powdered cuttlebone, or veterinary colloidal calcium.

LONG-TERM PROBLEMS

When tortoises are kept for periods of many years using husbandry techniques that prevent them from functioning totally as they would in the wild, long-term problems are caused. Frequently, because the progress of the problem typically is imperceptibly slow, symptoms can become gross before being noticed by the owner.

Such cases frequently are difficult to diagnose accurately, mainly because most tortoises kept in this way are suffering simultaneously from many problems.

Deficiencies

Vitamin, mineral, and trace element deficiencies are particularly difficult to diagnose. I know of no research work that has been done on the subject with regard to tortoises. It is, however, normally not necessary to be aware of the detail deficiencies. Getting the tortoise onto a diet with vitamin and mineral supplements designed for reptiles will solve most of these problems. Please note that vitamin injections rarely are effective.

Kidney Damage

If slightly inadequate thermal husbandry is practised over a long period

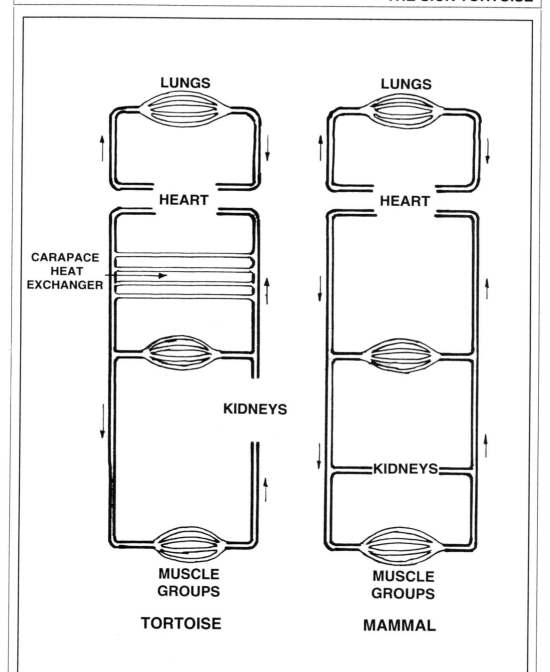

DIAGRAM SHOWING THE DIFFERENCES BETWEEN THE TORTOISE
BLOOD CIRCULATION AND MAMMALIAN BLOOD CIRCULATION.

(10+ years), kidney function becomes steadily worse and the kidneys eventually can become blocked and malfunction. When this happens, the blood flow through the back legs and tail is reduced to a tiny fraction of the normal flow. This situation causes the back legs to lose function, so the animal pulls itself along with its front legs. For obvious reasons, this normally is accompanied by anorexia. One normally can demonstrate that this muscle malfunction is not due to problems of the local nervous system by touching the underside of the feet. The tortoise should prove its nervous system is intact by withdrawing its apparently non-working leg.

Because the blood stream loop that flows through the kidneys also feeds the genital organs, any partial or total blockage of the kidneys will lead to a reduction of sexual behaviour and partial or total impotence.

The treatment for this is exactly as for anorexia, but the time needed to effect a cure obviously can, in some circumstances, be very prolonged.

Liver Damage

If tortoises are fed diets too rich in protein or diets containing milk products, liver damage will result. The major symptom of this is anorexia, but unlike "normal" anorexia, the tortoise does not lose weight and remains active, sometimes hyperactive.

This condition can be corrected by tube-feeding, then normal feeding with low-protein food. Anabolic steroid injections (see your veterinarian) help speed the regrowth of damaged tissue, but unless they are accompanied by a correction of husbandry, they will achieve nothing.

There are no miracle cures for this kind of problem. It generally is necessary to effect an immediate and dramatic improvement of the husbandry and to keep the animal alive by tube-feeding until the changed husbandry takes effect. Half-hearted changes in husbandry often are not effective with long-term problems.

With all long-term problems there is a point of no return, when so much internal damage has been caused that no cure can be effective. However, if one doesn't wait too long, is prepared to make the necessary changes, do the necessary work, and, above all, persevere, it is remarkable what sometimes can be achieved.

BLOOD TESTS

Tortoise blood can be sampled and tested just as can human and other mammalian blood. However, samples are more difficult to take and are more easily contaminated, sampling procedures cause the animals some distress, and most importantly, reliable guides to average values and the meaning of abnormal values are not widely available. For these reasons, blood tests are not used much in veterinary practise. However, the tests can be useful for some difficult diagnostic cases and for research purposes, so I have included the following list of blood sample results taken from nine active and healthy *Testudo graeca* during summer.

In anorexic tortoises, uric acid levels can increase two or three fold and blood urea levels can increase two or three hundred-fold.

If taking samples, thoroughly wash the tortoise to avoid sample contamination. In particular, it is important not to leave the slightest traces of urination on the

BLOOD TESTS			
Test	Average	Max	Comment
Urea (μmol/L)	1.8	2.6	main indicator of kidney function
Uric Acid (μmol/L)	599	965	
ALT (iu/L)	8.0	21.2	main indicator of liver function
AST (iu/L)	251	517	
Protein (g/L)	65.8	84.9	

tortoise's limbs as this would invalidate urea and uric acid readings. Remember that samples taken from the front limbs may differ from those taken from rear limbs, particularly if the kidney function is impaired. Remember also that taking samples from cold tortoises can be virtually impossible because the heart rate slows with body temperature, thus lowering the blood pressure.

IMMUNE DEFICIENCY

If a tortoise is kept using sub-optimal husbandry, its growth is retarded. There also is another effect: the tortoise's immune system becomes slowly but steadily less effective. If a tortoise is kept as a solitary animal in reasonably hygienic conditions, its impaired immune system seems to produce no difficulties for the animal whatsoever. The effect can be dramatic, however, if the tortoise is moved to a new home, particularly, although not exclusively, if it now is placed with "companions." The tortoise suddenly finds itself subjected to a variety of diseases that can progress very rapidly, and lethal results can be all too common.

If one acquires a tortoise that previously has been kept in northern Europe, look carefully at its growth rings and if possible find out about its past history from its previous owner. Try to get an impression if it is large or small for its age. If it is small, it is very likely to be immune deficient and will probably take two to three years of good husbandry to make good the problem. In the meantime, great care must be taken to avoid exposing the animal to potential disease sources.

Such tortoises are best kept solitarily. At the very least, avoid any possible contact with RNS carriers. This can prove very hard to cure and can turn into pneumonia very easily.

Any slight wound or scratch should be treated promptly and effectively since any delays can mean septicaemia and death.

Great care should be exercised with hygiene. Any sign of disease should receive prompt veterinary attention during this period.

If care is taken and the general husbandry is good, the tortoise will begin to grow at a normal rate and its immune function will return.

Captive penned tortoises. Tortoises kept in groups like this suffer considerable long-term hygiene and behavioural problems. Tortoises are naturally solitary animals.

THE LAW

There are three broad areas of English law that affect tortoise keepers. Other European countries have laws which are broadly similar, but differ in detail. American readers should note that American laws at the national, state, and local levels vary widely and must be checked for each individual case. Americans may want to read this chapter mostly for background information.

CRUELTY

Broad-based animal cruelty laws have been operative in England since Victorian times. In particular, the Cruelty to Animals Act of 1876 still applies and is regularly used. In principle, these laws apply to tortoises, and prosecutions under these laws have been successfully brought by the R.S.P.C.A., mainly against dealers. There is, however, a difficulty in bringing cases of cruelty against tortoise keepers. The husbandry advice available to tortoise keepers in the past has been so poor that any barrister defending someone accused could find a book recommending whatever cruel practise the keeper may have attempted. I hope this book will make this defence more difficult.

In my opinion, the following items constitute cruelty:

1) Drilling holes in the carapace, doubly so if general anaesthetic is not used. This causes pain when done and provides access beneath the protective surface to possible infections.

2) Tethering a tortoise, using either drilled holes or tethering a limb. A tortoise will never accept being tethered. Even after ten years it will continuously try to work free. The result of effective tethering normally is severe malformation of either the carapace or limbs.

3) Keeping a tortoise in a confined area with inadequate facilities so that the claws are worn down beyond the quick while trying to escape. Claws with normal wear will regrow quite rapidly, but claws worn down to nothing will never regrow.

4) Controlling hibernation tempera-

tures so poorly that a tortoise is blinded.

5) Keeping tortoises with dogs, particularly pedigreed dogs. Although most dogs ignore tortoises most of the time, horrific damage occasionally can be done. One doesn't keep cats and canaries in the same cage!

6) Any practise that fails to produce reasonably normal health, growth, and behaviour.

7) Failure to get an ill animal reasonably treated.

A court's opinion as to what constitutes cruelty may or may not differ from mine.

TRADE

There is an international agreement called CITES (Convention on Trade in Endangered Species). Signatory countries, such as the UK, are obliged to pass laws to control trade in earmarked species. *Testudo graeca* is legally classified as an endangered species, and as such it is illegal to sell, transport for sale, or advertise for sale any protected animal, alive or dead, in part or whole, without a license issued by the appropriate authority. In the UK the authority is the Department of the Environment (Wildlife Division) in Bristol.

The effect of this law is that one can legally import a tortoise from the wild provided that it is not subsequently sold, and provided that one obtains the appropriate licenses from EVERY country that it passes through, including the source country and destination country, plus a collection permit from the source country, plus agreement from the transporters...a mind-blowing bureaucratic solution!

There is a widespread misconception that importers and traders can't sell tortoises, but a tortoise owner can. This is not so because the law applies equally to everybody. Legally, it could hardly be otherwise. There is one difference—the D.O.E. normally will issue licenses to owners and breeders, but they normally will not issue licenses to traders and importers.

VETERINARY TREATMENT

In order to protect animals, there exists in England a legal monopoly for vets. In general terms this means that it is acceptable to carry out medical treatment to one's own animals but, except in an emergency, it is illegal for anyone other than a qualified vet to medically treat any animal he does not own. It is similarly illegal to diagnose illness in animals other than one's own. The basic statute is the Veterinary Surgeon's Act of 1966.

As far as mammals are concerned, this legislation is undoubtedly of great benefit since there is little doubt that vets have a monopoly of expertise. Unfortunately for birds, fishes, insects, and reptiles, only a few vets have the necessary expertise, and many animals suffer while owners search for appropriately qualified vets.

I make an open plea to the veterinary profession hierarchy—*please* make it easier for owners to find vets who have specialist knowledge in the treatment of various non-mammalian animals. At the time of writing, it is possible for members of the public to find only vets who are "willing to treat" tortoises and other non-mammalian animals. There is a difference—between being "willing" and being "able."

An over-calcified eggshell of *Testudo graeca*. Photo by the author.

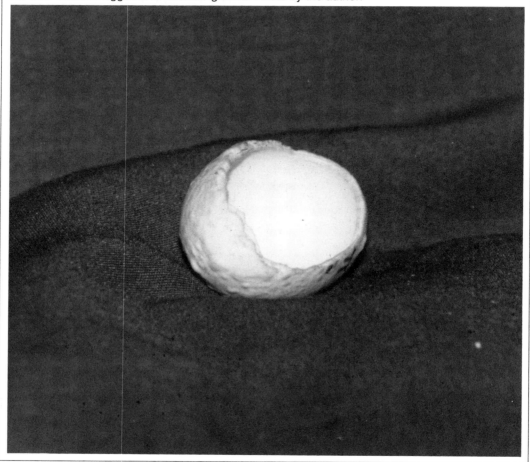

MEASUREMENTS & RECORDS

It can be shown mathematically that if a tortoise remains the same shape and density as it grows, then the ratio of weight to length cubed remains constant. Using weight measurements in grammes and length in centimetres, the average value of the ratio for a healthy adult *Testudo graeca* is 0.22.

It is not easy to always tell if a tortoise is skinny or fat, so this ratio is an excellent way of checking. The length used is the straight line carapace length measured over the nuchal scute and the supracaudal scute. Sometimes the plastron protrudes beyond the carapace, in which case use the straight line length measured over the carapace supracaudal scute and the plastron gular scutes. In either case, it is necessary to measure this length to an accuracy of one millimetre.

Regular measurements should be taken and records kept. The weight of a healthy, well-kept tortoise has an annual cycle. During hibernation it should lose weight, but only at an imperceptibly slow rate. For the first three weeks out of hibernation it should gain weight very rapidly as the gut fills. After these three weeks, there should be an approximate balance between food input and faeces and urine output, leading to a slow but steady weight increase throughout the summer. Then for three or four weeks before hibernation the tortoise stops eating and empties the gut, giving a fairly rapid drop in body weight.

If one compares the weight at any stage to the weight at the same stage last year, there should be an increase. The factors affecting the size of this increase are discussed elsewhere. In general terms, most adult tortoises kept in northern Europe grow too slowly because they are kept too cold. Most hatchling tortoises grow too quickly because they are fed diets too high in protein.

If a tortoise does not eat (for example because of anorexia) its weight falls as body fats disappear, but the carapace remains the same size. This means the W/L (cubed) ratio falls.

If tortoises are kept calcium-deficient for a large percentage of their lives, their carapaces become "pyramided." Such carapaces develop internal spaces that reduce the average density of the tortoise and hence reduce the W/L (cubed) ratio.

If an adult imported tortoise is simultaneously kept calcium-deficient and fed a diet too high in protein, its body grows but not its carapace. Excess body fats are laid down, mainly on the shoulders, making it impossible to fully pull the limbs and head inside the carapace. This increases the W/L (cubed) ratio.

A fit, healthy tortoise has a high W/L (cubed) ratio but appears to be slim, agile, and active, and can easily pull the limbs into the safety of the carapace.

If good records are kept, it is amazing how helpful they can be. For example, most disease problems cause tortoises to lose appetite. This frequently goes unnoticed, particularly if the tortoise is one of a group. The resulting change in weight, however, can be picked out even when no other symptoms are visible. This enables earlier treatment and/or isolation.

Similarly, if one knows a female is pregnant but does not have the time to watch, a sudden loss of 150 grammes in daily weighing will tell you to go out and look for the eggs.

When tortoises are hatched, their plastrons are folded, hence their length is short compared with the width. This results in a high W/L (cubed) ratio. Juveniles start plump and slowly change to the more streamlined adult shape. This is reflected in their W/L (cubed) ratios, which steadily decrease to the adult value when they reach sexual maturity at about five or six years (assuming good husbandry).

In addition to size and weight records, other records are a useful reminder that deworming may be overdue, that an illness has recurred from last year, and whether a particular treatment was or was not effective for a problem in the past. One always thinks at the time that one will remember the details, but it is my experience that although one remem-

The author raised *Alpha* from the egg and he is now (1994) eight years old (though he is shown here at 6 months). Photo by the author.

bers the broad outline of events, details become hopelessly blurred with the passage of time. There are no substitutes for written or computerized records. With the help of records you can continuously improve your techniques. Without records, you are groping in the dark. Almost all the information in this book is derived from observing, taking measurements, and keeping records.

TORTOISE RECORD SHEET   Sheet No _____

Species _____   Name _____   Egg No _____

Father _____

Incubation   Temperature _____° C   Mother _____

Humidity _____%   Date Laid _____

Days _____   Egg Weight _____gms

DATE	WEIGHT	LENGTH	RATIO	REMARKS

Suggested layout for a record sheet. Healthy tortoises should preferably be weighed weekly and sick tortoises weighed daily. Other measurements need only be taken two or three times a year. Problems, symptoms and medication should be noted when they happen. If it is necessary to take your tortoise to a vet, take all relevant record sheets with you — under some circumstances they can be very useful to him.

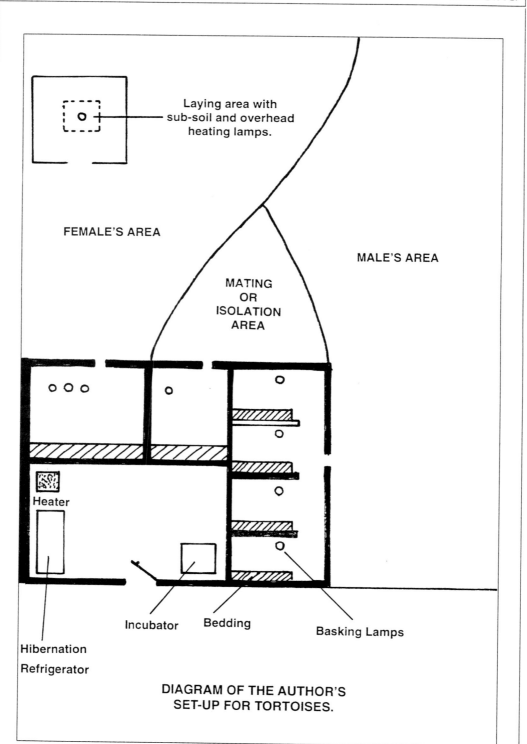

Laying area with sub-soil and overhead heating lamps.

FEMALE'S AREA

MALE'S AREA

MATING
OR
ISOLATION
AREA

Heater

Hibernation
Refrigerator

Incubator

Bedding

Basking Lamps

**DIAGRAM OF THE AUTHOR'S
SET-UP FOR TORTOISES.**

HOUSING

HOUSING A SINGLE TORTOISE

I have met many owners who appear to feel guilty about keeping a tortoise without a "companion." In my opinion, it is perfectly reasonable to keep a solitary tortoise, and it is infinitely better to do this than to obtain an inappropriate tortoise as a "companion." Tortoises are solitary, territorial animals. My experiments indicate that although individual animals have unique habits and preferences, in general a tortoise separated from its home range becomes agitated and eats less (it's unhappy?), while a tortoise separated from its "mate" appears untroubled and eats more (it's happy?). If you don't believe me, try an experiment yourself—convince yourself!

During the summer in England, it generally is not possible to keep tortoises healthy and thriving totally out of doors. It is possible to keep them healthy and thriving in an indoor vivarium, but unless the vivarium is very large and sophisticated this normally produces unnatural behaviour patterns and normally it appears to be more like factory farming than pet keeping—but that may be only personal bias.

I find that the best results are obtained using both indoor and outdoor areas. The tortoise can be moved from one to the other according to weather conditions, but this can be a considerable chore, so I prefer to allow a tortoise free access to either so it can make its own choice.

OUTDOOR AREA

Use as large an area as possible, preferably the whole of your garden. It generally is better to fence off plants that you don't want eaten rather than to fence off the tortoise. A pen on the lawn is *not adequate* for the following reasons:

1) Tortoises don't like being confined and will damage themselves on the usual wire netting boundaries while trying to escape.

2) Diseased tortoises pass infections to their surroundings and then reinfect themselves when they eat. The smaller the area the more likely are diseases and infestations to occur and the more difficult are such problems to cure.

3) Tortoises are prone to problems from the deficiency of a wide variety of trace elements and vitamins. The wider the range of plants and soils to which the tortoise has access, the less likely are such problems.

4) Unless the placement and construction of the pen are carried out very skillfully, it is unlikely to provide the best basking spots or hiding places available. The tortoise will find the best places if it is healthy and is given the chance.

5) Small areas normally produce unnatural behaviour.

FENCING

Perimeters **must** be escape-proof. Escaped tortoises usually are impossible to find and they cannot survive in northern climates without human help. For a tortoise, escape is a death sentence.

Walling—This is the best method. Barriers preferably should be brick or stone and at least 18 inches (45cm) in vertical height or 12 inches (30cm) with an overhang. Stone walls, as well as acting as a barrier, also reflect and store heat from sunlight and hence help the tortoise's basking efforts. Do not grow clematis or other climbing plants on outside walls—they can be climbed. Avoid corners with angles less than 90°. Some tortoises can climb these using "chimney climbing" techniques.

Wooden fences—These are less satisfactory because the bottom edge is always a problem. If there is a gap, the tortoise will squeeze through. If there isn't a gap and the bottom edge is touching the soil it will rot, then the tortoise will break through the rotten timber. One possible solution is to staple plastic trellis mesh along the bottom edge of the fence with about 4 to 6 inches (10-15cm) buried in the ground. Fencing *must* be inspected regularly and promptly repaired if necessary.

Hedges—These are totally inadequate.

Mesh fencing—This alone is not adequate for three reasons. First, healthy tortoises can climb it. Second, it causes accidents. Third, if a tortoise can see through a barrier it persistently will try to get through. If mesh fencing must be used, then sheet materials should be attached to make the fence opaque and unclimbable. Whatever method you use, it is important to realise that if you can succeed in forcing your fist through a potential gap using all your strength, then a healthy tortoise can get through that gap, as well.

Garden gates—These should be tortoise-proofed both by making them positively self-closing and by fastening lift-out boards across the gateway. This way humans can open the gate and then step over the boards, and the boards can be moved for wheeled access. It is my experience that this "belt and braces" approach is necessary, particularly so if children use the entrance. Unboarded gates invite both escape and accidents.

Plants—The garden should be made as much of a sun trap as possible, with continuous tall plantings on the north side and, if the plot is large enough, on the east and west as well. There should be a few shrubs for cover. Lavender and conifers are popular because the ground under them normally is dry, but the actual types of shrub are not critical. Leave an area with infertile soil to grow weeds. Cut down and remove these weeds from time to time to avoid any build up of fertility. This will encourage the growth of the types of weeds that tortoises eat.

A similar process can be carried out in order to produce a weedy lawn. In the spring cut the lawn and remove the clippings until the dandelions begin to grow. Then do not cut the grass until the dandelions have flowered and seeded, then cut and remove the grass. Repeat the process for clover. Do not use any fertiliser. Grass has short roots and grows best when the top 2 inches (5cm) of soil are fertile. This method reduces fertility and makes it easier for the weeds to compete with the grass.

Do not use weedkillers, insecticides, or herbicides; they are all poisonous and will damage your pets.

Soil—Light, dry, alkaline (limey) soil is best. Don't keep tortoises on waterlogged ground.

Contours—Tortoises like to climb and explore, and a rockery is ideal for providing interest and exercise.

Accidents—Do something about potential hazard areas such as ponds and concrete steps.

INDOOR AREA

This can be a garden shed, garage, or utility room. The area should be equipped with sleeping quarters for nighttime and a basking lamp for daytime, preferably with a timer. Some form of general air heating is necessary from time to time. Electric heating is best because it is clean and controllable, but it is expensive. Other equipment such as parafin or bottled gas heaters can be used, but ventilation is required exactly as for human use because such heaters give off potentially lethal gases. Space heating is very helpful, particularly in spring, and is essential for dealing with a sick tortoise at any time. The floor of this area must be able to be cleaned and disinfected conveniently. There are two straightforward methods.

Try covering the floor with a garden mulch such as "Forest Bark." When this becomes soiled dig it up and spread it on your garden. You will need a roofing slate or an upside down tray for feeding. Put it upside down to avoid directing urine onto uneaten food. This can be made to look very attractive and is particularly ideal for zoos. The method, however, can be a bit expensive, and if one has infection problems it can become a considerable chore and it is difficult to be 100 percent right with hygiene.

Another method is to cover the floor with a polythene sheet (obtainable from building merchants) and cover this with newspaper. This method is not so attractive, but it is less work and easier to keep hygienic.

Whatever method is used, faeces and urine should be removed daily and areas should be kept as clean and germ-free as possible.

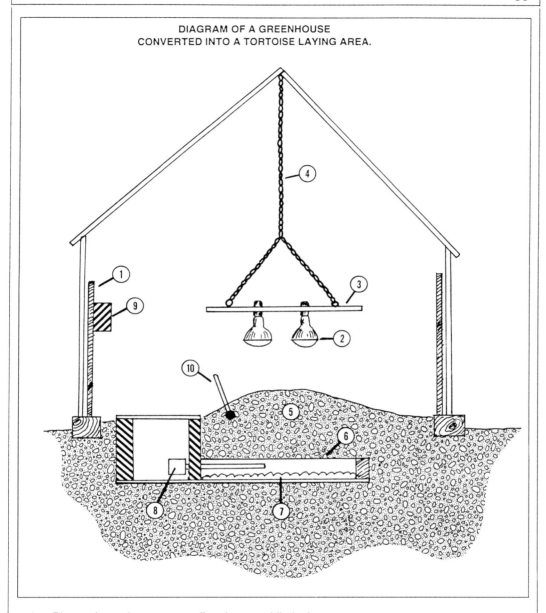

DIAGRAM OF A GREENHOUSE
CONVERTED INTO A TORTOISE LAYING AREA.

1. Plywood panels to prevent disturbance while laying.
2. Narrow angle heat and light reflector lamps.
3. Board to prevent the sunlight from changing the set temperatures.
4. Adjustable chain so that the lamp height can be moved to achieve 30°C soil surface temperature.
5. Mixture of soil and peat.
6. 2 feet x 4 feet metal box.
7. Soil heater is to be switched on constantly during the laying season.
8. Thermostat set to keep the main body of soil to 27° - 30°C.
9. Timer to switch on lamps during daylight hours.
10. Thermometer. Never use any heating device without a thermometer. Remember: If you can't count it, you can't control it. (After Bernardus, Duke of Wall.)

HOUSING FOR A GROUP OF FEMALES

This is, in general, no problem. Females will settle down happily in a group with shared facilities. A newcomer introduced into a group sometimes is badly treated by the existing residents, particularly if the newcomer is not in very good health. It therefore is advisable to have an extra area, complete with the necessary facilities, to use for isolation in these circumstances or for illness or injury. A second area also can be useful when deworming to avoid reinfestation, and also as a place to put the tortoises when cleaning out their normal quarters.

HOUSING FOR A GROUP OF MALES

Territorial, hierarchical, and sexual instincts can be very strong with healthy adult males, and the resulting anti-social behaviour can produce considerable problems. There are several ways of avoiding these problems.

1) Keep the group exactly as described for females, but with the tortoises at suboptimal health, fitness, and/or body temperature. Surely no one thinks that this is the best way? This method, however, commonly is practised—by default rather than design, of course. Owners frequently tell me that "My tortoises sit happily together." Females might, but I find that healthy, fit males walk, run, eat, climb, bask, explore, fight, sleep, but only rarely "sit happily!"

2) Provide an area sufficiently large so that a non-dominant male can escape from the territory of a dominant male. This is what happens in the wild, but the solution is impractical for most owners, because totally separate facilities would be required for each tortoise and the stocking needs to be less than about four males per acre.

3) Provide physically separate indoor and outdoor areas for each male. This obviously is effective, but it involves expense and a lot of fencing. This is an appropriate method for commercial breeding but is more like farming than pet keeping.

4) Provide separate but intercommunicating areas so that any individual can hide from his attacker. When hidden, he

needs to have access to bedding, basking, and feeding facilities. Under these conditions, the males seem to arrive at a *modus vivendi* relatively quickly and any scuffles tend to be infrequent and short-lived. It is even possible to stock more than one male per area provided that the occupants are reasonably evenly matched in fighting capabilities. It is essential with this type of setup to keep a check on the activities of the occupants and to prevent war, if necessary by blocking entrances between intercommunicating areas.

HOUSING MALES AND FEMALES OF MATCHING SUBSPECIES TOGETHER

If the area is large enough, the ratio of females to males is at least 2:1 (preferably 4:1), and adequate facilities are provided for basking and egglaying, such a group can be kept together and will behave relatively normally. It is essential to have an isolation area so that any male being a nuisance can be separated, particularly if females want to lay. If you keep tortoises this way, females should lay every year, and even if the males are removed, the females should carry on laying for many years. All, or nearly all, eggs laid should be fertile. If every female does not lay every year when kept this way, something is wrong.

When any of the "ifs" are ignored, the behaviour changes from normal, requiring more use of isolation areas to achieve normal eating, basking, and sexual behaviour. If abnormal behaviour is allowed to continue, the health of some or all of the tortoises will decline.

HOUSING MALES AND FEMALES OF THE SAME SPECIES BUT DIFFERING SUBSPECIES TOGETHER

Subject to the same "ifs" as the previous paragraphs, such a group can be kept together. However, most eggs will be the result of subspecies cross-fertilisation and will be mainly infertile. If several males are kept in such a group, one male often becomes dominant and as such impregnates all the females. Females matching the dominant male then will lay fertile eggs and other females will lay infertile eggs, subject to the in-built delays previously described. Although it is not unreasonable to keep tortoises in this way, it seems less than ideal because: 1) non-dominant males don't get a share of the females and get badly treated by dominant males; 2) many females risk pregnancy problems with no chance of viable offspring; 3) dominant males often spend so much time and energy interacting with other group members that they don't spend enough time eating and basking.

To minimise these problems, it is necessary to monitor the group constantly and take appropriate remedial action.

HOUSING DIFFERING SEXES AND SPECIES TOGETHER

This always causes some distress, behavioural problems, and pregnancy problems. The degree of the problems depends on the details of the mix. The worst possible mix is several *Testudo graeca* males and one *Testudo hermanni* female. This mix, in my view, constitutes cruelty.

GENERAL RECOMMENDATIONS

1) Keep differing species separately.

2) Keep females as a group in an area they can treat as home.

3) Keep males separate from females and either separate or separable from other males.

4) Carefully identify all your stock before putting a male and female together. Do not allow unmatched mating.

5) Try always to have a spare area with appropriate facilities available at all times for any emergency.

SECURITY

Since the CITES (Convention on International Trade in Endangered Species) trade restrictions have been in force, tortoises have come to be regarded as valuable and hence reasonable things to steal. Tortoises also always have been subject to impulse theft, mainly by children. In fact, it is stupid to steal a tortoise for two reasons. First, if a thief wishes to keep it, its survival chances are very low. Second, if a thief wishes to sell it, he needs a D.O.E. license.

I would, however, recommend all tortoise owners take anti-theft precautions. Photograph the carapaces of your tortoises with as much clarity as possible and keep copies of the pictures in a safe place. Carapace patterns are as distinctive as fingerprints. A photograph is important proof if ownership is disputed. Keep doors and windows of indoor areas locked. Use modern electronic alarm systems to warn of intruders.

OTHER SPECIES & OTHER PLACES

When tortoises, turtles, and terrapins (and for that matter all kinds of reptiles and amphibians) are sold by the pet trade, the information supplied by the vendors about species, sex, diet, climatic husbandry, country of origin, etc., is, in my experience, often wrong or not available.

This book has discussed, up to now, the problems of keeping hibernating tortoises in northern Europe. If you find yourself faced with the problem of keeping another species of tortoise, if you live in a different part of the world, or both, do not despair—this chapter is for you! I am afraid I cannot give you the kind of detail that I have given for *Testudo graeca*, because the experimental and zoological information available to me on other species is insufficient. I can, however, tell you how to set about finding the information for yourself.

Faced with an unknown chelonian, the first task is to decide about what species it is. Sometimes it also is necessary to know what subspecies it is. Most people try to ask a knowledgeable friend or pet shop owner what the species is. Unfortunately, there are about 350 different species of chelonians, and I find that even "knowledgeable" friends start to run out of knowledge after about 10 species. The only sensible way to decide is to use a good reference book and to have the animal with you as you check every characteristic. The only book at present in publication that comes close to covering the whole range is *Encyclopedia of Turtles* by Peter Pritchard, published by T.F.H. It takes a long time to check through all the characteristics of all the possible candidates before one can be sure that you have correctly identified the species, but it is vital to be right, so it is time well-spent.

Once the species has been identified it is necessary to identify the home range. "Pritchard" normally quotes at least one place where each species has been observed and generally gives a description of the animal's habits and diet. Using this as a starting point, geographical research normally will pinpoint the animal's native range. To do this one needs an atlas (or atlases) containing topographical, climatic, geological, vegetational and wind direction information. Given this information one can work out the home environment for any particular animal and, very importantly, how this particular animal uses the climate to achieve appropriate, consistent, year around body temperatures.

A FEW HELPFUL HINTS

Mountain ranges at right angles to prevailing wind directions normally have startling climatic differences between windward and leeward slopes. This means that a tortoise adapted to live on one slope generally will find life impossible on the other.

It is helpful to identify calcium sources. Tortoises cannot stray far from their source of calcium.

Temperatures fall with increasing elevation. Some tortoises find correct temperature conditions at sea level and some on elevated ground. All find large, high mountain blocks impassable.

Another important clue is the animal's feet. Examination of the limb and foot structure normally will reveal if the animal is terrestrial (cylindrical limbs), fully aquatic (flippers), semi-aquatic (webbed feet with claws), or marsh-living (enlarged feet).

When you have found out what the climate is in the tortoise's home range and also how the tortoise uses these conditions, you know what conditions are necessary to set up so that it can thrive. How difficult (and/or expensive) this is depends mainly on the difference between the tortoise's home climate and the climate where you intend to keep it. In the U.S.A. there are native chelonian species in all the states, including those adjacent to the Canadian border, but tortoises occur only in the southern parts of the country. Therefore, if an American citizen chooses to keep a species that is native to his state or if a resident of southern Europe chooses to keep one of the *Testudo* species, they should have minimal climatic problems. (There may, of course, be legal difficulties in doing this due to CITES or individual State legislation.)

Large climatic problems occur when there is a large difference between the home range and the captive range climates. If you attempt to keep tropical rain forest tortoises in Canada or attempt to keep hibernating tortoises in Brazil, you will have difficulties.

It is possible to overcome these difficulties providing one has the money, the common sense and is prepared to work out what is necessary. For example, it is feasible to build a heated, thermostatically controlled vivarium that could provide a steady 26°C to 30°C (79 to 86°F), shaded from the sun, with high humidity levels, which would be ideal for keeping tropical forest tortoises in a cold climate. Such a setup, however, would need to be very large if you wanted to get natural behaviour from the tortoises. It would be expensive to build and expensive to run, particularly when you realise that the constantly hot, humid conditions are a builder's nightmare because they are ideal growing conditions for all kinds of fungal growths and timber rots, and fungicides are likely to prove lethal to the animals you are trying to keep.

Giant tropical island tortoises present a virtually impossible challenge away from their home territory, partly because of the high temperatures required and partly because of the way they use wind and water for thermal regulation, but mainly because of the enormous scale of housing required to achieve anything approaching normal behaviour.

Another aspect of climatic husbandry that requires some thought is seasonal variation (or sometimes lack of variation). Most people seem to be aware of summer/winter temperature changes and make appropriate arrangements, but dry/wet seasonal changes and photoperiod changes seem to go unnoticed. To some species such changes are significant.

If a southern hemisphere tortoise is moved to the northern hemisphere or *vice versa*, the reversed seasons could well cause significant problems, particularly with breeding, until the animal becomes acclimatised to the changes. It is important to realise that although it is possible to acclimatise tortoises to change of climatic *timing* it is *not* possible to acclimatise tortoises to changes of climate.

The next thing you must think about is providing for the animal's behaviour patterns. If the tortoise buries itself overnight or for hibernation (as does *Testudo graeca*), then a spot should be provided so that this can happen. If the tortoise digs tunnels, appropriate digging areas should be available. If the tortoise uses tunnels dug by other animals then tunnels should be dug for it. Some have unusual and unexpected requirements. For example, Pancake Tortoises (*Malacochersus*) hide in rock fissures and then expand the distance between plastron and carapace so they are jammed in and predators can't pull them out.

Hingeback (*Kinixys*) tortoises come from tropical rainforest areas where the rivers frequently are steeply banked and fast flowing, so the tortoises obtain water by channelling rainwater into their mouths through gutters in their carapaces.

Take nothing for granted! Try to find out as much as you can about the particular species you are trying to house.

One thing that seems to take humans by surprise is that tortoises in general are solitary. Most fare better if kept with access to large areas. Keeping any species of tortoise as though it were a herd animal can lead to problems. Problems generally also occur if differing species of tortoise are kept together. Oddly, however, tortoises will co-exist reasonably well with a wide variety of non-tortoise species.

You need to think about breeding and/or the effects of suppression of breeding. Specifically you need to think about provision for mating (or preventing mating), provision for egglaying, provision for egg incubation, provision for hatchling care.

You need to think about disease and hygiene. In particular, whatever housing is used it is essential that cleaning and disinfection can be carried out easily and efficiently whenever it proves necessary. If you keep more than one tortoise, an extra isolation area often can save a lot of work and, frequently, tortoise lives if disease should strike.

Diet varies from species to species, and some American species even change their diet as they grow older, so one cannot generalise. However, there is a tendency for owners to feed diets that would be more suitable for human than tortoise consumption. In general, most people tend to feed a diet too short of fibre, too high in protein, and much too low in calcium. Think carefully about the appropriate diet. Watch the tortoise's growth rate, fatness or thinness, and carapace growth. Be prepared to change the diet if any of these appear abnormal.

USEFUL ADDRESSES

IN ENGLAND

British Assn. of Tortoise Keepers
c/o Edgbaston Hotel
323 Hagley Road
Birmingham, B17 8ND

Tortoise Trust
BM Tortoise
London WC1N 3XX

British Herpetological Society
c/o Zoological Society of London
Regent's Park
London NW1 4RY

Assn. for the Study of Reptilia and Amphibia
c/o Cotswold Wild Life Park
Burford
Oxfordshire OX8 4JW

IN AMERICA

National Tortoise & Turtle Society
P.O. Box 9806
Phoenix, Arizona 85068-9806

Chicago Herpetological Society
2001 N. Clark St.
Chicago, IL 60614

NOAH
Dept. Biology
Case Western Res. Univ.
Cleveland, OH 44106

New York Turtle & Tortoise Society
163 Amsterdam Ave., Suite 365
New York, NY 10023

In Europe, land-dwelling chelonians are called **tortoises;** sea-dwelling chelonians are called **turtles** and freshwater-dwelling chelonians are called **terrapins.**

In America most chelonians are called **turtles.** A few exceptions are called tortoises. This can lead to confusions. This book uses the European names.

The vast majority of the experimental work done by the author has been done with two Mediterranean species, *Testudo graeca* and *Testudo hermanni*. Both of these species are land-dwelling, vegetarian, hibernating tortoises. Much of what is written will also apply to other species, but careful thought is required before one can assume that any particular fact will apply. There are obvious differences needed in husbandry of non-hibernating species, fish-eating species, water-dwelling species, etc.

American towns with climates approximating to that of the climate of the home ranges of *Testudo graeca* and *Testudo hermanni* are New York City, Toledo, and St. Louis. The nearest equivalent to the English climate in the USA is Seattle.

SUGGESTED READING

TT-013

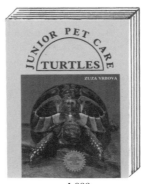

J-009

H-1011

PB-129

CO-026

KW-051

*T.F. H. Publications
has many good books about
turtles and tortoises.
Those books are available
at pet shops everywhere.*

M-515

TW-132

PS-307

SK-034